THE LOGIC OF

Howard Taylor

British Library Cataloguing in Publication Data:
A catalogue record for this publication
is available from the British Library

ISBN   978-1-871828-69-6

Typeset in 11 pt Garamond
and published in 2009 by
The Handsel Press
at 35 Dunbar Rd, Haddington EH41 3PJ
handsel@dial.pipex.com

Cover design and printing by
West Port Print & Design Ltd, St Andrews (01334 477135)

Thanks are expressed to the Drummond Trust
of 3 Pitt Terrace, Stirling,
for assistance with the publication of this booklet

Contents

It remains true, in my experience at least, of the events of my lifetime that the moment a society consciously begins to reject Christianity and its values and, for whatever reason, begins pursuing the opposite, the most startlingly evil practices appear once more to emerge from dark corners and flap their hideous wings abroad.

Lord Hailsham, *The Door Wherein I Went*, p. 48
(however see also his seemingly opposite
sentiments at the end of Chapter 3)

Preface – Right and Wrong

All systems of ethics that I have encountered make the assumption that human life on earth is valuable and therefore should be preserved. But actually there is no ground for this assumption in secularism which denies that we may know that there is an overarching purpose for our human lives.

But does this mean that any religion will provide the ethical teaching we need?

Islam, which bases its belief on the Koran, teaches that this life of finite length is only a test for an infinitely long life in paradise or hell. Life on earth has no value in its own right.

The Bible which teaches us that we are made in the image of God and that He, in Christ, the Eternal one, has identified Himself with our finite earthly life, does give value to this life – a value which comes from our Creator. Other religions may teach us that the Divine commands us to love our neighbour, or even our enemies, but the Bible tells us that God Himself loves His enemies and we should be like Him.

This, dependence on a Creator who loves us, was assumed in the years of science's advance and there has been no discovery which contradicts it. Yet the view that there is no purpose to the existence of the cosmos dominates much of science today. This blind faith is having an unintended but devastating effect in Western society.

This sorry state of affairs is partly (but not entirely) the responsibility of the Church which, as the New Testament warned,[1] has not behaved well especially towards the Jews – the human subject matter of the Bible. This was especially true when the Church wielded considerable power and/or influence.

Secularism and Islam have been strengthened by this misuse of power and influence by the Church. In its Catholic and High Church forms it has claimed a unique status in the eyes of God among the other Churches, and has become addicted to ritual – bordering on the idolatrous or even the superstitious. In its Liberal forms it has simply given in to the prevailing moods of the day informed by the media. In its Conservative Protestant forms it has either become legalistic

---

[1]   E.g. Romans 11:18-22.

or it has simply trivialised the gospel in its 'happy clappy' styles of worship. Of course there are exceptions, and, in spite of these failings, the light of Christ, through the Church in its various forms, shines on.

In spite of what is said above, secularism is a myth. In its crusade against Christianity it is sucking in alternative 'spiritual' worldviews such as militant Islam.

I hope the subsequent pages will do their small part to dispel the secular myth.

Acknowledgements

Peter Loose of Chelmsford first pointed me to the web site *www.naturalism.org* and that provoked me into writing this piece.

I am particularly grateful to Dr Henry Haslam author of *The Moral Mind*, for his criticism and suggested re-wording of many sections of this book as well as his very careful overview of the manuscript. Dr Thomas Torrance with whom I once taught Moral and Social Philosophy gave me encouragement as did his uncle the Revd David Torrance who gave much help with regard to publication. Thanks too go to the Scottish Order of Christian Unity for considerable financial help and support. The publisher, Revd Jock Stein, who chose the title, gave me much practical advice.

To all of them I am most grateful and last but not least there is my wife Eleanor whose enthusiastic look at the chapters inspired me to go on.

With all of this help one must be grateful but the faults of this book are mine alone.

Howard G. Taylor
August 2009

Introduction
Faith and Reason

Much of the Western World has been dominated by beliefs in human dignity; the equality of all races; universal access to education; universal access to health care; and also democracy for all. Although all of this is good, we must not take it for granted. There is growing cynicism. There can be no rational basis for any of these beliefs unless there is also a belief that human life on earth has real value (independent of an individual's opinion or that of a particular society) – a value which comes from a transcendent reality that created us for a purpose. There may be individual opinions supporting these beliefs, but they will be devoid of rational foundation unless there is at least an implicit acknowledgement that there is a transcendent purpose for which we exist. Without a belief in purpose (other than individual opinion which may or may not believe in purpose), there can be no *lasting* (down the generations) belief, in value. At the time of writing there is increasing concern about websites that promote, with some success, suicide among the young.[2] Unless there is a common belief in value, the efforts of governments, which want to stem the tide of bad behaviour, will be doomed to failure (however imaginative their efforts). It is reported in a recent edition of the Daily Telegraph[3] that there is a Conservative-Labour report which is calling upon the two party leaders to address the issue of social breakdown in Britain. The answer is not to revive the Church in its many forms because its behaviour, past and present, can provide little inspiration. This is true of the Church in all of its many denominations – both ancient and modern. It is the message of God and His everlasting love that needs to be made known.

But which god? I believe that the goodness of the actual Creator shines through all His creation and therefore all peoples everywhere have a universal agreement about what is good and what is evil (though their customs might differ on relatively small points). There are no people who regard cheating as good or kindness to the needy as evil. Therefore any religious teaching that goes against these views must be wrong. If the founder of a religion believed human life on earth had no value or that people were born into different racial groups – some privileged, some not – then we would know that this religion

---

[2]   For example see the report in the Times on 26th January 2008.
[3]   15th September 2008.

was wrong in its teaching about God. If a religion taught that the true God is everlasting love then this would correspond to what we all intuitively know.

It seems reasonable to believe, assuming there is a transcendent world (which will be shown in this book), that at the heart of this transcendent world there is a Person (because he cannot be less than us). It also seems reasonable to believe that this Person is very great love (after all most of us know a little of love). Love is always self-giving and therefore the Cross, in which the transcendent world experiences human suffering, death and the consequences of human sin, stands at the heart of human history. 'God was in Christ reconciling the world to Himself.'[4] The Resurrection, quickly following the Cross, guarantees that death and human foolishness will not have the final say in the destiny of the world.

Because he is a Person, our knowledge of him must be personal, i.e. not subject completely to law and contract, but rather based on trust which itself is based on hearing or reading what a person says (his word) and speaking to him (conversation or prayer). This is how we know any person. Household rules may be useful and needed, but obeying them is not what the relationship between parents and children is all about. Law is meant as a restraint against evil during the time when our personal relationship with God is imperfect. Personal trust is primary and eternal, and law, though given by God as a temporary expedient, is secondary. So often in the Church's history, the Church has made law primary and grace there to enable us to keep the law. But this is wrong. It is the relationship of grace and faith that is all important. A good illustration of this is Jesus' own words when He said, 'The Sabbath was made for man, not man for the Sabbath'.[5] There is a Sabbath law but it must not be so elevated that it gets in the way, stopping the proper relationship between God and humans to develop.

The Church is commissioned to give this message to the world but she herself has not really lived up to it, having succumbed to many of the evils of humankind. In one way this is not really surprising since the Bible itself predicts it.[6] Nevertheless this does not mean that the basic message of the Church cannot be trusted. One thing that we should note is that this fact actually bears witness to the grace of God because despite the appalling faults of the Church down the ages, the gospel is, through the Church, being accepted today in many lands where it was not known before.

Most people in the world intuitively recognise that there is more to life than mere atoms and laws of physics – more, that is, than naturalism, materialism

---

4   2 Corinthians 5:19.

5   Mark 2:27.

6   See for example Acts 20:29.

or physical science, can describe. The physical may well be important and be part of what a human being is eternally but there is more to life than that which is open to physical investigation. Science is good, but is not all embracing, because there is more to life than an examination of the physical can describe. People may not be able to articulate it, nevertheless they recognise their conviction as true. That is why religion (good or bad) is so widespread in the world. Attempts to remove the Judaeo/Christian heritage from any country will create a spiritual vacuum which will inevitably suck in other less pleasant forms of spiritual belief. However it is my conviction that the recognition of a transcendent world should be respected, even though some of the manifestations of religion may be harmful.

There is only one way of knowing the transcendent world, and that is by faith, because 'scientific' methods will be inappropriate to examine that which cannot be defined in terms of atoms and natural laws. Faith, it is said, believes in things without evidence. Is that true? Rather, faith is entrusting one's life to Something for which – although it is unseen (by us) – there is ample evidence that **it** exists.

There is such a thing as faith without evidence. Physical science examines physical things, therefore it could never show that non-physical things don't exist. It has been very successful in examining physical things. It could hold the lesser view that the physical world is entirely self-contained. However, it could never reach that view unless it had reached a theory of everything (TOE). Not only has it not reached that point but, as will be seen, mysteries about the physical world's behaviour increase (not decrease) the further physical science advances. Some have claimed that Gödel's Incompleteness Theorem shows that, in principle, a TOE can never be reached. But in spite of all this, many people continue to hold to naturalism – the belief that only physical things exist – or that non-physical realities are not needed to explain the physical world.

Yet however successful physical science has been in explaining some of the physical world, it does not follow that the physical is everything in nature or creation. That is a faith without evidence – so this kind of blind faith does exist after all!

The 17th century French mathematician and philosopher, Pascal, said:[7]

Men despise religion. They hate it and are afraid it may be true. The cure for this is first to show that religion is not contrary to reason, but worthy of reverence and respect. Next make it attractive, make good men wish it were true, and then show that it is:

- Worthy of reverence because it really understands human nature.
- Attractive because it promises true good.

---

[7] Pensées (12).

Many people will think that this is written in response to Richard Dawkins' *The God Delusion*. That is understandable but wrong. It was written long before that book hit the press. Nevertheless I do really think that Richard Dawkins is both mad and bad. Anyone who thinks that extremely complex systems like the most primitive forms of life (before the alleged processes of evolution could get started) are the result of some cosmic fluke is mad, and anyone who says human life has no purpose (and therefore no value other than individual opinion which may or may not believe in purpose) is bad.

In this book, Chapter 1 demonstrates that the belief that an analysis of the physical world can reveal all knowledge, is not only without evidence, it is also incoherent and that is true however far science advances.

Chapter 2 draws on that religious sceptic Bertrand Russell. It begins to reflect on those questions that Bertrand Russell considered most important for the human race – questions which cannot be answered by science or philosophy.

Chapter 3 continues with those questions especially as they relate to right and wrong.[8]

But Richard Dawkins might ask, as he has often done before, 'Which god – Zeus for example?' Chapter 4 seeks a reason for believing the Bible's revelation. It is a reason that is not often given but is truly external to the Christian Faith. I leave it to the reader to judge the validity or otherwise of the case made.

Some people have no response to the scientific or philosophical issues raised in much of the book but their problem is the one of evil and suffering. I give a short (though I hope not facile) response to this most troubling of troubling questions in chapter 5.

Bertrand Russell according to one modern philosopher tried to reduce everything to impersonal constituents.[9] He also claimed he could not know anything. In my view these two points are connected. Both mind and matter have at their base something deeply personal. I try to illustrate the necessary very personal nature of scientific discovery in chapter 6.

This theme is continued in chapter 7 when I illustrate the engagement with God using the Lord's Prayer.

Some may protest that I engage 'modernism' but not 'postmodernism'. Postmodernism uses reason to show that 'reason' itself is invalid. But any system which is arrived at by reason and then uses reason to invalidate reason must be self-refuting. Nevertheless postmodernism is right in saying that there is no

---

8   An April 2008 article in the Daily Telegraph (*In a land without morals it is no wonder that children kill one another*) raises the issues.

9   Bertrand Russell, *My Philosophical Development*, page 194.

room for reason in the 'modernist/atheist' worldviews. In my view only theism can be reconciled with human reason, so I will use reason to argue against materialist atheism.

So much of the book raises the question '*What is a human being?*' This question is much in people's mind when they consider the question of genetic manipulation as it relates especially to humans. The issue of bioethics is raised in the first appendix.

The second appendix relates to the question of evolution. If the theory of evolution is true it makes life more comfortable for the atheist but does not prove his position. However he desperately holds on to it even in spite of the difficulties. The second appendix considers Richard Dawkins' exposition of this theory as found in his book explaining it for the layman. This writer is very unconvinced as he explains in this appendix.

The third appendix is a continuation of the former as the Intelligent Design movement is considered.

The final appendix considers the mind-brain problem (considered in this book) as it is discussed by the Oxford mathematician Roger Penrose.

Who is the book meant for? The thinker and seeker that comes to it holding any worldview but with an open mind.

Throughout, much of history the search for knowledge has assumed that there is more to reality than can be described by the analysis of the physical world. Materialism was a minority belief. Sadly this has changed. No evidence has been found for the change but the change dominates much scientific thinking. This relatively new belief is without evidence – so a belief without evidence dominates the way we are taught to think. This faith without evidence must be challenged. That is the purpose of this book.

Chapter 1
Why Naturalism Must Fail

Faith is the great cop-out, the great excuse to evade the need to think and evaluate evidence. Faith is belief in spite of . . . the lack of evidence. (Richard Dawkins)

Naturalism is the philosophical viewpoint which holds that everything has a natural cause in the material universe, because it says there is nothing else but the physical world. It denies the existence of anything supernatural or spiritual or transcendent. Specifically, it denies the existence of God. According to naturalism, moral values and aesthetic values can be nothing more than a state of mind. Absolute, objective values, if they exist at all, must be grounded in the physical world because there is nothing else for them to be grounded in. According to Naturalism all moral values (such as those based on the value of human life; all beauty (such as Mozart's music, the appearance of a rose, or mountain grandeur), can be reduced to the movement or arrangement of the observer or listener's atoms and molecules – real goodness and real beauty being the products of the human imagination, which itself is a state of the physical brain and/or the nervous system.

That is not to say that belief in God or any god is necessary for people to be really good or to really appreciate beauty, but that such concepts can have no rational ground apart from the reality of God. It is quite reasonable to believe that the 'light' of God 'shines' through all creation so that most people intuitively value goodness and beauty whatever their theoretical worldview. And therefore we find much goodness around us even if it is being slowly eroded.

There is no evidence, and could be no evidence, to prove this belief that only physical things exist, but it is still propagated as if it were definitely true.

If it is generally believed to be true, or if the God of love and goodness is replaced by an unpleasant god, then dire consequences will eventually envelop humanity.[10]

How could the physical sciences demonstrate that the non–physical does not exist? Some people may choose to believe that it does not exist, but that is what it is – a personal choice. They may claim that they are not convinced by the evidence that there is something beyond or outside the physical, but that does not mean that the evidence does not exist. Naturalism is a matter of personal faith: it is no more than that. And it is a rather dismal faith, too, demeaning to human beings and the universe we inhabit.

If I say: 'There has been an insect in this room', I am stating that I have noticed evidence of a particular insect in one place in the room. You might, by looking where I am looking, dispute that claim and we could have an investigation and discussion. However if I said: 'There is no insect in this room', I would be making a different kind of claim. I would be claiming that I had searched the whole room – under the cupboards and behind the curtains for example – and I have reached the conclusion that there is no possibility that an insect, however tiny, could have escaped my notice.

If I say there is no God, I am implying that I have searched the physical universe and all other possible unseen aspects of reality – and that would seem to

10   For example among very many see 'New figures reveal hidden epidemic of self-harm'. (Independent newspaper, 27th July 2004)

be impossible. If I make the claim that God may exist but has no effect on the physical world with which I am familiar, I am claiming that I understand all effects and causes in the physical world. I could only be this confident if I knew that physical science had finished, or nearly finished, its work of exploring the physical world in terms of purely physical causes. Not only has science got nowhere near that position, but it is exposing more, not less, mystery the farther it advances. The more we learn, the more we realise how much more there is that we do not understand. Claims have been made in the past that we are close to knowing all that there is to know – and they have been proved false. For example, in 1900 Lord Kelvin, one of the great scientists of his day, said, 'There is nothing new to be discovered in physics now. All that remains is more and more precise measurement'. There were many distinguished scientists at the time who took a similar view to this, but his bold pronouncement was soon followed by Relativity Theory and then Quantum Mechanics, both of which were to explode outmoded ways of thinking.

If it really were true that our human lives are simply the result of physical processes, then there could be no overarching purpose for our existence. That is because purely physical things don't initiate purposes. A bridge, for example, has a purpose that we have given it. It does not, itself, initiate any purposes. If there is no overarching purpose, can we believe that human life has any value? Something without purpose (either useful or aesthetic or perhaps possessing sales value) is soon discarded.

Hence the denial of absolute purpose is bound to lead to a sense of loss of value and therefore a gradual loss of reverence for one another. It won't happen immediately because vestiges of respect and value will remain for a few generations after the sense of purpose has gone.

It could be argued that 'natural selection' and evolution explain our will to live, because without such a will our species would die out. However even if this theory be true, once we had realised that the value put on human life was only a survival strategy of our genes – as alleged by evolutionary theories – there being no intrinsic value to human life, we would lose our respect for one another. There would be no reason to reverence another. We would still have our natural desire to survive – thus suicide would still be uncommon – but telling the potential suicide victim his worth beyond his immediate relationships which he/she values (if any) would be fruitless.

I sometimes ask my students, 'If I were to come into this classroom and say that I did not believe that human life had any value, what argument would you use against me?'

If they simply say we 'feel' that human life is valuable, I would say in return, that there have been many people in history who have not believed in the value of human life. They were relying on their feelings too! So how do we show that our feelings are more in tune with reality than their feelings?

If we wish to hold on to morality but without a belief in ultimate purpose,[11] what are our reasons for so doing? There is no point advocating moral living unless moral values are real and human life itself is of value, and how can these values be based on nothing more than the physical universe? How can moral values be proved by science? If human life has no purpose the belief in its value will have no basis in reason. We may find that it is in our interests to behave well towards others, just as other animals do, but that is not the same as developing and applying our moral sense.

Naturalism is a belief that dominates many of the Western World's education systems.[12] Influential people routinely ridicule alternatives such as belief in God or the reality of the human soul or spirit.

To recap, naturalism is a philosophy for which, in principle, there can be no evidence. Yet it is harmful. This is because, without a reason for living beyond one's own preferences, there is a danger that moral values may not survive for long. So naturalism's dominance of our culture may lead to a continuing erosion of the belief in a real goodness that exists independently of our personal opinions – private or collective. This means that the objectivity of moral values is lost. Consequently, we see ethical confusion and the break down of right behaviour in all levels of society. Surely intelligent people who promulgate secularism must realise this. If that is the case, they bear enormous guilt for the consequent suffering of young people in our Western society as all that could give them love and security – for example marriage and the family – breaks down. No wonder the Muslims in our society are angry! I believe theirs is a mistaken creed, but nevertheless their frustration at the dishonest arguments to support Western secularism, with its tragic consequences, is more than understandable.

However it is beyond dispute that much goodness remains in many ordinary people. My own conviction is that this is because the goodness and beauty of God (recognised or not), pervading the world, means that ordinary people in all countries do recognise goodness and beauty when they see them and hope for them in their own lives. This will be true unless their sense of goodness and beauty has been negated by (for example) selfishness or fear, or by an evil ideology that has taken over their lives – be it religious or non-religious.

---

[11] Nietzsche called this '*The English Fantasy*'.

[12] It is interesting how, at the time of writing, there is a passionate desire from many to keep the teaching of the many problems with evolutionary theory outside the classroom.

'Naturalism.org' is the website of prominent people who actually hold to this view. Its advisory board includes such influential names as Susan Blackmore, Nicholas Humphrey, and Daniel Dennett.

Naturalism is the understanding that there is a single, natural world as shown by science, and that we are completely included in it. It introduces itself with the words in italics quoted below. I have interspersed my brief comments in ordinary text.

What evidence could there be that only things examined by physical science exist and that science is the only way of knowing anything? Physical science examines physical things. It therefore cannot tell you that non-physical entities don't exist. Actually there is a mass of contrary evidence, as we shall see.

Naturalism holds that everything we are and do is connected to the rest of the world and derived from conditions that precede us and surround us. [Again, what is the evidence for this conviction?] *Each of us is an unfolding natural process, and every aspect of that process is caused, and is a cause itself. So we are fully caused creatures, and seeing just how we are caused gives us power and control, while encouraging compassion and humility.*

This contradicts itself. For if everything we do and think is caused by the previous distribution of particles/energies in nature, then we would have no power to decide to do or to be anything including the power to make ourselves humble or compassionate. We would be slaves of the impersonal laws of physics.

By understanding consciousness, choice, and even our highest capacities as materially based, naturalism re-enchants the physical world, allowing us to be at home in the universe.

This comment makes the assumption that we know how consciousness arose. But up to the present day there is no theory of how 'consciousness' emerged from the biology of vegetation. Karl Popper is widely recognised as one of the twentieth century's greatest philosophers of science. He has said: 'The emergence of all consciousness, capable of self reflection, is indeed one of the greatest of miracles.'[13] That still applies in the twenty-first century, and is a live issue. 'No metaphysical problem is discussed today more vigorously than that of mind and body.'[14] One of the most significant problems of the understanding of the mind is how its consciousness arose.[15]

There could be no 'choice' if everything I do and think is materially caused. If physical law caused all my thinking, how could I, by thinking, decide that your thought was more or less correct than my thought? If all thinking was

---

[13] *The Self and its Brain*, page 129.

[14] From an Article in *Encyclopaedia Britannica* – 1997 edition.

[15] Closely related to it in humans is the issue of thought and reason which is briefly referred to in the next paragraph.

materially caused how could I 'understand' anything? There would be no way to weigh up the relative merits of one thought and another thought – certainly not by thinking, since that too would be materially caused. If naturalism were true we could not know it was true – in fact we could not know anything at all!

Nietzsche, who grasped this last point, realising its significance, rejoiced in the contradiction it contained. He wrote:

> As for the superstitions of the logicians, I shall never tire of underlining a concise little fact which these superstitious people are loath to admit – namely that a thought comes when it wants, not when 'I' want; so that it is a falsification of the facts to say: the subject 'I' is the condition of the predicate 'think'.[16]

In other words, in an age of dramatic scientific discoveries we decide that we know nothing!

To the obvious question: 'How can it be true that there is no truth?' Nietzsche provides no answer. He cannot. Instead he enjoys the irony that the rationality that made science possible has been destroyed by science.

It is not simply that we are no longer sure that the presuppositions of logic are justified, but that science has made them impossible to justify.

So we have the Nietzschean circle:

- Science provides the given – a self-understanding we must live with
- This has made our normal understanding of scientific truth unintelligible.

The only way out of this irony is to acknowledge what most people have instinctively known, namely that physical nature is not the whole story and that naturalism cannot be true!

Perhaps science could tell us that all physical effects have physical causes. That would be a lesser goal than proving that non-physical entities don't exist, but nevertheless it would be relevant to this discussion. I have mentioned it briefly above. There could be no evidence for even this lesser view unless we could show that the physical universe is a closed system of cause and effect – nothing non-physical affecting what goes on in it, such as a non-physical human mind of thought. If physics provided us with a TOE (Theory of Everything) it would have gone a long way to reaching that goal. However, there are problems with this:

---

[16] *Beyond Good and Evil*, Section 17 p. 47. By 'superstitions of the logicians' he meant the beliefs of those philosophers and scientists who think they are free to think!

1 The further science advances, the greater the mystery that it uncovers

For example, the discovery of the DNA double helix was a great leap forward in understanding the biology of life, but it left the mystery of how such an information-rich molecule was formed in the first place. It was the discovery of the nature of the simplest form of life or self-replicating molecule (before the alleged processes of evolution could get started) that forced the famous atheist Anthony Flew to give up his atheism and embrace the old argument from 'design'. He says:

> It seems to me that Richard Dawkins constantly overlooks the fact that Darwin himself, in the fourteenth chapter of *The Origin of Species*, pointed out that his whole argument began with a being which already possessed reproductive powers. This is the creature the evolution of which a truly comprehensive theory of evolution must give some account. Darwin himself was well aware that he had not produced such an account. It now seems to me that the findings of more than fifty years of DNA research have provided materials for a new and enormously powerful argument to design.[17]

Commenting on Flew's change of mind, Dr Jonathan Witt writing to the Times (22 December 2004) says:

> Peering into the world of even the simplest functional, self-reproducing cell — the thing Darwinism needs before it can even begin to work — Flew finds a world of intricate circuits, miniaturised motors and enough digital code to fill an encyclopaedia. Natural selection can't build this bit by bit. It needs life first. Nor can the natural outworking of the laws of nature. Flew and the rest of us are waiting for a detailed, credible description of how such complexity occurred without design. Bold assertions, prestigious degrees and hand-waving don't count.

A recent edition of the Encyclopaedia Britannica says:

> A critical and unsolved problem in the origin of life is the origin of the genetic code. The molecular apparatus supporting the operation of the code, the activating enzymes, adapter RNAs, messenger RNAs, and so on are themselves each produced according to instructions contained within the code. At the time of the origin of the code such an elaborate molecular apparatus was of course absent.

So, as noted above, an advance in knowledge (in this case the discovery of DNA) leads to more mystery, not less.

---

[17] The Associated Press, New York, Dec 9, 2004.

There are many other examples from science of how its advance in real knowledge has forced us to face greater questions than hitherto could be imagined. Quantum theory is another example. It has exposed the sub-atomic world as non-picturable. This sub-atomic world (of electrons etc.) seems to behave in ways that are counter-intuitive. It can be described by mathematics but we do not know what an electron actually is – is it a little hard or soft thing? It is neither. So what is it?[18] We don't know, but everything in the physical world is made of such tiny packets of wave/particles. We are made of trillions and trillions of them.

There seems to be no evidence whatsoever that the advance of science is closing the vast gaps in our knowledge of the physical world. Quite the opposite, in fact.

2 Gödel's Incompleteness Theorem

In the 1930s the German mathematician Kurt Gödel showed that there will always be statements in formal systems of mathematics that cannot be shown to be true or false from within those systems. Each system would start with the given axioms which could – applying fixed procedures of logic – be used to test certain theorems to decide or prove whether they were true or false. He managed to translate statements about mathematics into mathematics itself. He then showed that it was possible to use mathematics to say something about itself. He managed to number the statements in a formal system of mathematics in such a way that statement number n said, 'Statement number n cannot be proved in the system.' We can see that this statement must be true, for if not, statement number n would have a proof, i.e. the system would contain a flat contradiction. The same is true if it could be disproved within the system: the system contains a true statement, which it cannot prove or disprove. From an enlarged system – with more axioms and more procedures – it could be seen that n is true or false. But that enlarged system again would itself contain its own undecidable statements, and so on . . . So if Mathematics is incomplete, so must the universe be – a universe with Mathematics as its foundation. This point and similar points are argued by John Barrow, John Polkinghorne, Paul Davies and Stephen Hawking.[19]

---

[18] Bertrand Russell wrote: 'It is not always realised how exceedingly abstract is the information that theoretical physics has to give. It lays down certain equations which enable it to deal with the logical structure of events, while leaving it completely unknown what is the intrinsic character of the events that have the structure ... All that physics gives us is certain equations giving abstract properties of their changes. But as to what it is that changes, and what it changes from and to – as to this, physics is silent'. (*My Philosophical Development*, p. 13)

[19] See, for example, Stanley Jaki's paper 'A late awakening to Gödel in Physics'.

Definite Knowledge

The famous sceptical philosopher (already referred to in a footnote), Bertrand Russell, wrote in his *History of Western Philosophy*, 'All definite knowledge belongs to science'.[20] That sounds like the faith of those holding to naturalism. Why is it illegitimate to make such a statement? The statement itself cannot be proved by any scientific observation or experiment. So if it is true it is not true! It therefore refutes itself and must be false. Similarly one often hears a statement to the affect that 'all knowledge comes through measurement and testing.' For the same reasons that too refutes itself and is nonsense.

There is a real knowledge with which we are all familiar, but it is not scientific This is **friendship.** Friendship leads to knowledge of other persons – a genuine knowledge of realities. Such knowledge could not be obtained by science. I could never know 'you' by examining your body and brain in a medical laboratory. But I could know the real 'you' – who certainly exists – by making friends with you. You could tell me what you are thinking about (a holiday in Switzerland for example). I could never learn that by examining your neurons. I might see the result in your neurons of your imagining the mountain scenery but I could not 'see' the famous Matterhorn mountain in colour and cloud as you imagine it.

However if you really are my friend and, with reason, I trust your word (i.e. I have *faith* in you), then I could learn what is going on in your mind which is something real that has real consequences in the material world. (For example it moves your body – which is at least physical – to the travel agent to book a holiday). Thus we can gain knowledge of a reality by non-scientific means – a knowledge we could not gain by science.

Therefore there is more to reality than can be accessed by science.

The Self

Thus, the 'self' that is you cannot have a purely physical make-up examinable by physical science. Those who hold to naturalism deny the existence of anything but the physical. Hence some (or all) of them hold the absurd belief that there is no self. So naturalism.org tells us:

> The self: As strictly physical beings, we don't exist as immaterial selves, either mental or spiritual, that control behaviour. Thought, desires, intentions, feelings, and actions all arise on their own without the benefit of a supervisory self, and they are all the products of a physical system, the brain and the body. The self is constituted by more or less consistent sets of personal characteristics, beliefs, and actions, but it doesn't exist apart from those complex physical processes

---

[20]   P. 13.

that make up the individual. It may strongly seem as if there is a self sitting behind experience, witnessing it, and behind behaviour, controlling it, but this impression is strongly disconfirmed by a scientific understanding of human behaviour.

Although they claim that their conclusion is based on a 'scientific understanding', in fact it is based solely on their naturalist assumption. A truly scientific approach would look at the evidence before making unsubstantiated assumptions.

The naturalist argument has to go: 'My physical composition is changing all the time, as some atoms and molecules are discarded and new ones are incorporated into the tissue of my body, so there is no real continuing "me" that once went to pre-school. That was someone else that no longer exists – and it wasn't me that robbed a bank ten years ago so I am safe from prosecution! Not only has the actual substance of my body changed but its patterns have too – except for my DNA. Even that is now doubtful because recent research shows that my mental states may switch on and off certain codes within the DNA.'[21]

Even if this were not the case, could I identify myself with my genes? If I could, I would be 99.9% you because that is the proportion of my genes that I share with another person. But you and I might be quite different! People share 70% of their genes with bananas. Does that mean that a banana is 70% human?

Actually this argument applies to the identity of most things. For example if, over time, I replace every brick in my house, one by one, it might still be considered the same house. This little example shows there is more to identity that just physical make up. The identity of my house is given to it by me who lives in it and my neighbours who know it. So who or what gives me my identity so I can truly say that I really did go to pre-school?

One of the supporters of naturalism is Susan Blackmore, and she has an internet link to 'Who am I?'. On her own logic, the answer to her question should be 'Well, no-one actually', because no self exists. This was/is the view of Buddhism, to which Susan Blackmore expresses some allegiance. The belief in 'no self' finds its classic statement in the ancient Buddhist text, *The Questions of King Milinda*, where, in answer to the king's first question, the monk Nagasena denies that the self exists – and therefore concludes that he (Nagasena) does not exist! However if one clicks on Susan Blackmore's link 'Who Am I?' one gets a fairly normal description of her life and achievements. Her self certainly seems to exist, even though her body, brain and memories are constantly in flux.

---

[21] See for example the article by Sharon Begley in the *Wall Street Journal*, June 21, 2002.

So what is the self? Can it have a purely naturalist explanation? Definitely not! Even though the nature of the self and all subjective experience and consciousness remains a great mystery, naturalism cannot give a satisfactory explanation and must ultimately fail.

The fact that anything exists at all is a great mystery. However, we do know that we as persons exist and our minds exist. Furthermore, there must be something that exists that is not finite, to which everything else which is finite ultimately owes its own existence. All finite things owe their origin to other finite things. Thus they too owe their existence to yet other finite things. Assuming this process is not infinite[22] we must reach the point where we meet Something which itself is not dependent on anything for its existence, because it had no beginning and is itself infinite.[23] Either impersonal particles/energy waves or laws of physics are those ultimate infinite things or there is Something beyond the physical world that is eternal. The Universe of atoms and laws of physics cannot be this eternal thing because it gives the impression that is dependent and not infinite. For reasons that should become clearer as we go on, I would go as so far as to say that this Eternal 'thing' must be Eternal Mind and therefore cannot be spoken of without using a personal pronoun.

It must be reasonable to think that what lies behind all things cannot be less than personal because we personal beings have arisen in the universe. But is there a way of knowing that is appropriate for knowing Mind – a way that is probably different from the all-important reductionism of the natural sciences?

Whatever we believe about ultimate reality we cannot escape mystery.

So who made God? This question is the essence of Richard Dawkins' argument on page 141 of *The Blind Watchmaker*.[24] He says that a Creator, in order to make such a thing as DNA, would have to be at least as complex as DNA. If we have to explain the origin of the DNA's complexity, then we must explain the origin of the complexity of God.

The flaw in this argument is that it assumes that the laws of nature (i.e. cause and effect) apply to that which is beyond nature – a patently false assumption. If God exists then he is, by definition, beyond nature.

---

[22] Bertrand Russell did think the process might be infinite. However an infinite series of physical causes does seem far more inconceivable than one Infinite being.

[23] This is the ancient Cosmological argument for the existence of God. One can read arguments supporting it and criticising it most textbooks on Philosophy. I recommend *Questions That Matter* by Edward Miller.

[24] The whole book is reviewed in Appendix 2.

Dawkins goes on to say:

You have to say something like 'God was always there', and if you allow yourself that sort of lazy way out, you might as well just say 'DNA was always there', or 'Life was always there'. and be done with it.

Although, no doubt Dawkins means this as a rhetorical sentence, its rhetoric can only be effective if the sentence makes any sense. But it doesn't. It is beyond dispute that DNA and life were not always there. No one pretends that they were. This is something that is amenable to the usual scientific process of reasoning from the available evidence. We do not know the laws that relate to the eternal existence of God who is beyond nature, but what we do know is that life has not always existed.[25]

Chapter 2
Questions Without Answers

Bertrand Russell posed a series of questions which he deemed to be the most interesting and important for humanity.[26] If he is right about their importance, the questions must be about reality, for it would be hard to argue that questions about anything that doesn't exist could be of supreme importance. He also says that they cannot be answered in the 'laboratory' nor by 'philosophy' (which can only discuss them), but can only be answered by 'theology' if it exists (Bertrand Russell believed it didn't). This leads to his paradoxical view that the most interesting and important questions facing humanity have no answers.[27]

He writes:

. . . all dogma as to what surpasses definite knowledge belongs to theology. But between theology and science there is a No Man's Land . . . this No Man's Land is philosophy. Almost all the questions of most interest to speculative minds are such as science cannot answer, and the confident answers of theologians no longer seem convincing. These are:

• Is the world divided into mind and matter, and, if so what is mind and what is matter? Is mind subject to matter, or is it possessed of independent powers?

---

[25] I give another response to this often asserted Dawkins argument at the end of the 'Philosophy' section in the appendix on Intelligent Design.

[26] Introduction to *History of Western Philosophy* and also p. 789.

[27] A related group of questions comes from Richard Dawkins, although he predicts there will, one day, be an answer given by science. He asks: 'Why are the laws of physics the way they are? Why are there laws at all? Why is there a universe at all?' (Guardian newspaper 8th February 2008)

- Has the universe any unity or purpose? Is it evolving towards some goal?
- Are there really laws of nature, or do we believe in them only because of our innate love of order?
- Is man what he seems to the astronomer, a tiny lump of impure carbon and water impotently crawling on a small unimportant planet? Or is he what he appears to Hamlet? Is he perhaps both at once?
- Is there a way of living that is noble and another that is base, or are all ways of living merely futile?
- If there is a way of living that is noble, in what does it consist, and how shall we achieve it?
- Must the good be eternal in order to deserve to be valued, or is it worth seeking even if the universe is inexorably moving towards death? . . .

To such questions no answer can be found in the laboratory . . . The studying of these questions, if not the answering of them, is the business of philosophy.

We begin with his first question and divide it into two – the nature of mind and the nature of matter – and we turn to Leibniz, whom Russell regarded as one of the greatest minds of all time.[28]

What is mind?

Leibniz, in what Professor Anthony O'Hear (President of the Royal Institute of Philosophy) refers to as his 'telling image',[29] reasoned that the mind couldn't be identical to the physics of the brain. His argument went something like this. If your brain was as big as a windmill, I could walk inside it. I would meet much physical activity but one thing I would not meet would be an idea or a thought. So although I might see much movement in the neurons and could possibly, using a science of the distant future, deduce what you are thinking about, I could not actually 'see' or 'hear' or 'read' directly what you are thinking about – say a snow-covered and cloud-covered Matterhorn with the wind whistling about its peak and notices warning the climbers of the dangers ahead.[30]

---

[28] The only other person who receives this honour from Russell is Pythagoras.

[29] *After Progress*, p. 241.

[30] Leibniz's actual words are: 'One is obliged to admit that *perception* and what depends upon it is *inexplicable on mechanical principles*, that is, by figures and motions. In imagining that there is a machine whose construction would enable it to think, to sense, and to have perception, one could conceive it enlarged while retaining the same proportions, so that one could enter into it, just like into a windmill. Supposing this, one should, when visiting within it, find only parts pushing one another, and never anything by which to explain a perception. Thus it is in the simple substance, and not in the composite or in the machine, that one must look for perception.' (*The Monadalogy*, paragraph 17)

Physical systems behave in certain ways – and not other ways. What they do is neither true nor false; it is just the way things are, the whole story of purely physical phenomena. Our human *descriptions* of physical activity may be true or false but the activity itself is neither. For something to be true or false it must be the product of a conscious mind. We who are conscious can have thoughts about physical phenomena. These thoughts of our conscious mind may be either true or false.

When water boils at 100°C at sea level, it is not correct or incorrect behaviour for water – it is just the way things are. That is true for all physical phenomena. Just as water does not consciously know anything (such as its own boiling state), no combination of physical phenomena is conscious. Advances in the study of the brain may be impressive but they only show how physical effects have other physical effects. They may show where, in the brain, reasoning (or morality or religion) have their effect, but they don't show what the reasoning actually is about!

However, my thoughts can be correct or incorrect. I plausibly may think that the square root of 1000 is 35. However, that thought is incorrect. The square root of 1000 is actually approximately 31.62. By doing the calculation I can consciously correct my thought.

Now if the mind is just a complex combination of physical causes and effects[31] it would be inappropriate to describe any of its operations (in producing thoughts) as true or false, just as it would be inappropriate to describe the boiling point of water as true or false.[32] Only conscious thoughts can be true or false.

Bertrand Russell again:

> If we imagine a world of mere matter, there would be no room for falsehood in such a world, and although it would contain what may be called 'facts', it would not contain any truths, in the sense in which truths are things of the

---

[31] Appendix 2 of this book deals with this subject in more detail.

[32] If a computer gives a wrong answer to a calculation, it is not because its mechanism is breaking the laws of physics, it is rather that the software programmer or the computer user (who have used their minds) have made a mistake. Mistakes are made by conscious beings that can have thoughts. All thinking is conscious. Even a broken down computer giving the wrong answer is not making a mistake since the answer it gives is due to a failure of its mechanism not a failure of its conscious thought. It isn't conscious. If it is to be corrected it will be the result of a computer programmer and his mind consciously working on it. Even if it has a self-correcting mechanism it will be the result of a sophisticated IT expert applying his conscious mind to the mechanism. However our minds, not being governed by physical laws, can ponder their own thoughts and therefore correct themselves.

same kind as falsehoods. In fact, truth and falsehood are properties of beliefs and statements: hence a world of mere matter, since it would contain no beliefs or statements, would also contain no truth or falsehood.[33]

O'Hear comments:

> How is it that some bits of matter can both react in physical ways and experience, from the inside as it were, what is going on? It cannot just be a matter of one bit of the brain monitoring or controlling other bits, like a thermostat in a heating system, for the thermostat, though certainly part of the system and reacting to other parts, is not itself consciously aware of anything.[34]

You know directly what you are imagining even if you know nothing about neurons and the workings of your brain. So your access to your thoughts must be different from that of a scientist who is looking at the workings of your brain. Thus your mind, which can think about your thoughts, cannot be identical to your physical brain. This relates to what we have said about the 'self' above.

Here is a another comment from O'Hear about the theory that mind and brain are the same thing.

> No progress whatever has been made on this problem, *[of trying to understand mental activity as physical activity]* despite thirty or more years of intensive effort, probably because the very notion of the mind being the brain is at root unintelligible.[35] *(His emphasis)*

Your thoughts affect the physical world – they may encourage you to go to the Travel Agency and book a holiday – and therefore they are certainly real. So we have something that is real but not physical. Once again, therefore, naturalism fails.

What is matter?

Leibniz reasoned that if matter is made of particles of finite size then each one could be broken in two and thus not be fundamental. So if matter is made of particles they must be infinitely small. However since a definition of matter is that it occupies space then matter cannot be made of matter! It must be made of other non-material things. Leibniz called them 'monads' or 'souls'. Modern people might say that matter comes from energy. However, that does not solve the problem since energy is *matter* in motion or potential motion. Modern quantum theory is proving Leibniz's argument correct as it discovers a rather counter-intuitive ghostly world of atomic phenomena. So theoretical physicist Paul Davies can edit a book on Quantum Theory and call it *The Ghost in the Atom*.

---

[33] Bertrand Russell, *The Problems of Philosophy*, p. 70.
[34] *After Progress*, p. 242.
[35] *After Progress*, p. 171.

So what is everything made of? Perhaps modern theoretical physics has the answer. But does it? As reported in an earlier footnote, Bertrand Russell said:

> Nothing whatever in theoretical physics enables us to say anything about the intrinsic character of events . . . All that physics gives us is certain equations, giving abstract properties of their changes. But as to what it is that changes, and what it changes from and to – as to this, physics is silent.[36]

This remains true to this day.

The Biblical worldview is that God created in stages. That means that we should expect detectable discontinuities in the created world, which is examined and discussed by scientists and philosophers.

What are these detectable discontinuities?

First, the nature of matter which we have discussed above. It will never be possible to reduce it to the 'nothing' from which it emerges.[37]

Second, the nature and origin of life, which involves information not reducible to the physics and chemistry of the matter from which it is composed – but rather needs a mental input, as it seems does all information and language; for example if palaeontologists find ancient writing in a cave they will not assume that it was the product of natural sources but that somebody wrote it. This applies to the Search For Extra-Terrestrial Life, where a form of language or code that is not reducible to natural law (such as a sequence of prime numbers), is being looked for.

An important part of the argument is that the complexity of the simplest form of life contains information in the form of 'code' or 'words' or 'language' (DNA and RNA, for example).

The atheist Richard Dawkins writes:

> What lies at the heart of every living thing is not a fire, warm breath, nor a 'spark of life'. It is information, words, instructions . . . Think of a billion discrete digital characters . . . If you want to understand life, think about information technology.[38]

Third, the nature of mind and consciousness, which relates to 'mind' and, as we have already seen, cannot be reduced to matter or vegetable life.

---

[36] *My Philosophical Development*, p. 13.

[37] An electron emerging in a vacuum according to the logic of Heisenberg's uncertainty principle is not an electron emerging from absolutely nothing.

[38] *The Blind Watchmaker* p. 112.

Fourth, the nature of reason, by which we think abstractly and universally. This is probably limited to human and divine thought. Humans can think of things with which they have had no physical relationship: the past, the future, and objects far away. We can think of things that we have never interacted with materially and things that don't even exist, such as 'golden mountains' or unicorns.

Humans too can think of things in general such as the nature of dogs, democracies, and buildings. Such universal concepts do not exist as concrete things. (For example we can talk about philosophical theory.) It was this thinking ability that made Pythagoras and later Plato realise that there must be a transcendent world that enabled universal reason to exist. Although most of us think that Plato's solution of a transcendent world of 'ideas' is unsatisfactory, Plato did at least recognise a problem that troubles philosophers to this day.[39]

A human being can also ponder his/her own life, death, and possible life after death, and be aware of good and evil. We can know that we are responsible (partly) for our behaviour. Even those holding to the worldview of naturalism know that, though their official beliefs deny it.

Information

Underpinning the first two (at least) of these detectable discontinuities is information. When we consider matter/energy as a wave or field we find that it is a wave understandable by mathematics. Galileo is reputed to have said, 'Mathematics is the language with which God wrote the universe'.

In one of his non-religious books on quantum theory (*Quantum Theory – A Very Short Introduction*) John Polkinghorne says it is intelligibility rather than objectivity from which all physical existence emerges.

So seemingly information lies in and behind all physical reality.

The theoretical physicist Paul Davies in *New Scientist* recently wrote:

Normally we think of the world as composed of simple, clod-like, material particles, and information as a derived phenomenon attached to special, organised states of matter. But maybe it is the other way around: perhaps the Universe is really a frolic of primal information, and material objects a complex secondary manifestation.[40]

(Rather than the other way round: information emerging from mindless particles and energy.)

---

[39] Bertrand Russell remarks that the problem has never been solved. It troubled his atheism all his life as did his necessary rejection of 'objective morality', from which he could never free himself, even though he saw it as being inconsistent with atheism.

[40] January 30, 1999, p. 3.

This resonates with the Bible's teaching that 'Word' is the foundation of all things. Bertrand Russell wrote, in *Study of Mathematics*:

Mathematics, rightly viewed, possesses not only truth, but supreme beauty – a beauty cold and austere, like that of sculpture, without appeal to any part of our weaker nature, without the gorgeous trappings of painting or music, yet sublimely pure, and capable of a stern perfection such as only the greatest art can show. The true spirit of delight, the exaltation, the sense of being more than Man . . . is to be found in mathematics as surely as in poetry.

Paul Dirac, who won a Nobel Prize for his work on quantum theory, wrote:

. . . fundamental physical laws are described in terms of a mathematical theory of great beauty and power . . . One could perhaps describe the situation by saying that God is a mathematician of a very high order and He used very advanced mathematics in constructing the universe.

Dirac's brother-in-law Eugene Wigner, winner of the equivalent of a Nobel Prize for Mathematics, spoke of the 'unreasonable effectiveness of Mathematics'. It is, he said, 'a gift, which we neither understand nor deserve.'

In the Spring 2005 edition of *Science and Christian Belief* there is a marvellous article by physicist Peter Bussey ('Beyond Materialism – Aquinus, Duns Scotus and Quantum Physics') making a similar point about matter. He likens the old mind-brain problem to mind-matter. It is mind that gives matter its form in terms of 'laws of nature'. Without form there would not be formless matter: there would be no matter. It is a brilliant article linking consciousness, quantum theory, a realist view of mathematics, the mind, and the laws of nature, with the nature of matter itself.

He comments that while biologists are looking for more physical explanations for biological complexity, physicists are looking to non-physical mind to explain matter itself!

When we press the question far enough, do we really think that we understand any physical processes in terms of other physical processes – say one pebble hitting another? The electrons, which supposedly surround the nucleus in the atoms of the pebbles, are not tiny hard or soft things. So what are they? They seem to emerge from non-material information.

Information in the form of mathematical code or something equivalent to languages must have its origin in Mind. If you receive a letter written in a language or mathematical code, you cannot discern the origin of the language or code from the chemistry of the ink or paper. Its message is explained not by the chemistry of the ink and paper but the mind who wrote it.

Einstein said:

We are in the position of a little child entering a huge library, whose walls are covered to the ceiling with books in many different languages. *The child knows that someone must have written those books.* It does not know who or how. It does not understand the languages in which they are written. The child notes a definite plan in the arrangement of the books, a mysterious order, which it does not comprehend but only dimly suspects.[41] *[emphasis added]*

This resonates with the Biblical teaching that God creates by His Word and upholds all things by the Word of His power.

This does not mean that God is part of His creation. We have to be careful to distinguish between Creating Word and created information.

In his book intriguingly entitled *In Praise of Idleness* Bertrand Russell confesses: 'I am not a materialist'.[42]

Now we jump to Bertrand Russell's last question. (We shall return to the others later.)

Must the good be eternal in order to deserve to be valued, or is it worth seeking even if the universe is inexorably moving towards death?

This raises the question of meaning. Something has meaning if and only if a purposive personal agent or group of such agents endows it with meaning and significance. To have meaning of any kind, a thing must be brought under the governance of some kind of purposive intention, whether an intention to refer, to express, to convey, or to operate in the production of some acknowledged value. This is true of all meaning. Meaning is never intrinsic; it is always derivative.

Objective or Subjective Meaning?

Some philosophers advocate a 'do-it-yourself' approach to questions of meaning. According to this view there is no 'objective' meaning of life waiting to be discovered. If we order our lives around things we desire, value and enjoy, within the structure of goals we take for ourselves, we render them meaningful and thereby give meaning to the life they compose. A person's life can therefore have 'subjective' meaning – or so they say.

Problems for Subjective Meaning

How do you distinguish between one kind of 'meaningful' goal and another? Someone may focus his whole life on collecting matchbox covers and another on finding cures for terrible diseases. (How does one distinguish trivial from *meaningful* goals? There is nothing to appeal to.)

Someone may be very good at torturing people and enjoy it very much so that he focuses his life on that pursuit. How does one distinguish between worthy goals

---

[41] Quoted by David Bodanis in *E=mc2* (emphasis added).
[42] In his essay *Scilla and Charybdis, or Communism and Fascism*, on page 72 of his book referred to in the text.

and unworthy goals? There is nothing to appeal to. How can a purely subjective approach to life's meaning account for these objective differences?[43]

If one holds with the naturalists that we have come from nothing, are here by chance, and are going to nothing, there can be no rational basis for believing that our lives have meaning or value.

Life everlasting by itself does not bestow meaning. A few thousand years watching television would not give meaning to our lives.

One of the alternative views about life everlasting also renders the meaning of life *on earth* null and void. For example if we hold that the next life (in heaven or hell) is infinitely long then this finite life loses all value except as a test for the next life.

If however we hold the Christian view that the Eternal Mind who created us for Himself actually meets our physical lives on earth (in Christ) then our earthly life which He values, takes on enormous value and meaning. This 'intersection' of the Eternal Divine life with our earthly lives is vitally important for meaning.

We move on to another of Russell's questions.

Has the universe any unity or purpose? Is it evolving towards some goal?

Naturalism is clear. There is 'no ultimate purpose'[44] or, as TV's favourite atheists Dawkins and Atkins often tell us, we must not ask the 'why?' question because it assumes there is a purpose.

However those who deny the validity of the 'why?' question have to say that the universe is in being and that is all there is to say. For them the only appropriate question to ask of nature is the 'how' question. How do natural phenomena occur?

But is the 'why?' question so silly?

Surely there must be other questions that follow the 'how?' question. The first one is surely the 'what?' question. *What* brought the Big Bang into being? (Assuming, for the sake of argument, that that is how the universe got started.[45]) What lies behind (if not before) it? Even granted that the Big Bang is the beginning of time, this is still a very real, obvious and legitimate question to ask. However when we begin to think about it, the 'what?' changes to 'who?'

---

43 I owe the wording of the above three paragraphs on 'meaning' to Thomas V Morris, *Making Sense of It All*, which is a study of the thoughts of Blaise Pascal.

44 www.naturalism.org

45 Not everyone in the secular scientific community accepts the Big Bang theory on the origin of the universe. See for example the open letter now signed by over 200 scientists originally published in *New Scientist*, May 22, 2004. Whatever turns out to be the correct theory on the origin of the universe, the fundamental metaphysical argument outlined here still applies.

It seems reasonable to believe that since personal beings exist, that which brought the universe into being cannot be less than personal. 'What?' has to change to 'who?'. Once we have begun to ask 'who?' then the 'why?' question of purpose naturally follows. Professor T F Torrance tells us that in 1929 Einstein said that science has now reached the stage where it cannot be satisfied simply with describing *how* nature is what it is in its ongoing processes, but must press on to ask *why* nature is what it is and not something else.

At these very fundamental levels of enquiry when we have reached the boundary of the natural world, the questions 'how do things behave as they do?' and 'why do things behave as they do?' converge into the one question. Once we have accepted the validity of the 'why?' question we have admitted that there may be purpose to the existence of the universe. If nature and our lives might have purpose then it is beholden upon us to seek that purpose so that we can discover how we should behave in this world. The universe forces us not only to consider what *is* the case but what *ought* to be the case and what *ought* to be our part in it.

Torrance has further made the point that science has operated with a false dualism between these two questions which has led to a false separation between the natural and moral sciences. It is this false distinction between the 'public world of facts' and 'the private world of values' that Lesslie Newbigin so ably challenged in his book *Foolishness To The Greeks*.

At the time of writing, the scientific establishment is complaining about the declining interest in science shown by school and university students. It is hard for such departments as Physics to recruit the students they need. This is certainly a sad and serious problem. But if it is the case that there is no purpose to the universe, then can we wonder that young people don't see the point or purpose in exploring the wonders the natural world contains, and instead simply turn to the utilitarian subjects which will make them more money?

Although natural science by itself cannot answer the 'why?' question it is the irrational denial of the legitimacy of the 'why?' question of purpose that is, in the long term, the greatest enemy of science.

It would be a great sadness for our human condition if we lost interest in discovering the wonders of nature. One of the mysteries of the human mind is that it possesses an intelligence and way of thinking that seem just right to be able to grapple with nature so as to uncover its inner logic – and this doesn't look to be the sort of thing that could have an evolutionary explanation. That is to say, the ability to understand abstract concepts such as quantum theory and the structure of the atom (say) seems irrelevant to evolution as simply 'the survival of the fittest'.

Paul Davies says:

> . . . we find that nature's order is hidden from us, it is written in code. To make progress in science we need to crack the cosmic code . . . What is remarkable is that human beings are actually able to carry out this code-breaking operation, that the human mind has the necessary intellectual equipment for us to 'unlock the secrets of nature' . . . It would be easy to imagine a world in which the regularities of nature were transparent and obvious to all at a glance. We can also imagine another world in which . . . the regularities were so hidden, so subtle, that the cosmic code would require vastly more brain power than humans process. But instead we find a situation in which the difficulty of the cosmic code seems almost to be attuned to human capabilities . . . The challenge is just hard enough to attract some of the best brains available, but not so hard as to defeat their combined efforts and deflect them onto easier tasks. The mystery of all this is that human intellectual powers are presumably determined by biological evolution and have absolutely no connection with doing science.

The following convictions (consciously or unconsciously held) would surely promote and help the flourishing of science:

1   The natural world is orderly and therefore open to rational investigation.

2   Its rational order is open to understanding by the human mind.

3   Nature's order is a contingent order. That is to say, its rational structure did not have to be as it is but was chosen to be as it is. If the orderliness of nature were simply the orderliness of mathematics (where such truths as 3 times 4 = 12 are not dependent upon anything but are necessarily true), then the rational structure of the universe could be discovered by mathematics alone. Further observation and experiment would be unnecessary. However if we believe that its order was 'chosen' to be as it is then observation and experimentation are necessary to delve deeper into its own rationality.

4   The natural world is good. Belief that it is evil, might make us try to understand it as we might try to understand the tactics of an enemy but there would be no joy in, or love for, the subject. Belief that it is neither good nor evil would rob its study of real purpose.

5   There is hope for the natural world. Even though it contains much suffering, the conviction that it will finally be redeemed by the love of its Creator, strengthens our desire to love and know its secrets. The Incarnation and Atonement are the great seals of God's affirmation of His redeeming love for the physical world which He will not finally forsake.

Now Bertrand Russell's next question:

Are there really laws of nature, or do we believe in them only because of our innate love of order?

Although Kant believed that our minds impose their own order on the nature that we observe, science assumes that there are discoverable laws of nature, intrinsic to nature itself, that govern the behaviour of physical objects. Their existence, though, poses a mystery that cannot be answered by nature itself.

The self-confessed materialist and Pulitzer Prize winner, Edward Wilson in his book *Consilience* skirts the related question: 'Why is the universe ordered?' with the words, 'fortunate comprehensibility of the universe', and with a description of the world as 'surprisingly well ordered'.[46]

Einstein, speaking of the 'miracle' that the universe is ordered and therefore comprehensible says:

> And here is the weak point of positivists and professional atheists, who feel happy because they think they have pre-empted not only the world of the divine but also of the miraculous. Curiously we have to be resigned to the miracle without any legitimate way of getting any further.[47]

This expresses his amazement that the laws of physics, which our minds are somehow attuned to understand, apply not just here on Earth but also in the remotest galaxy. Newton taught us that the same force that makes apples fall holds the Moon and planets in their courses. We now know that this same force binds the galaxies, makes some stars collapse into black holes, and may eventually cause the Andromeda galaxy to collapse on top of us. Atoms in the most distant galaxies are identical to those we can study in our laboratories. All parts of the universe seem to be evolving in a similar way, as though they shared a common origin. Without this uniformity, cosmology would have got nowhere.[48]

Now the next question of Bertrand Russell.

Is man what he seems to the astronomer, a tiny lump of impure carbon and water impotently crawling on a small unimportant planet? Or is he what he appears to Hamlet? Is he perhaps both at once?"

Here I am going to turn to the old familiar argument from Design. Before this is dismissed let me quote Bertrand Russell again, as he comments on this argument:

> This argument *[the argument from design]* contends that, on a survey of the known world, we find things which cannot plausibly be explained as the product of blind natural forces, but are much more reasonably to be regarded as evidences of a beneficent purpose.

---

[46] P. 50. (See my critical review of this book in *Philosophia Christi* (Volume 4 No. 1, 2002).

[47] From a letter by Einstein to Maurice Solovine, quoted by John Templeton in *The God Who Would Be Known*.

[48] I owe this paragraph to http://www.firstscience.com/site/articles/rees.asp

He regards this familiar argument as having no 'formal logical defect'. He rightly points out that it does not prove the infinite or good God of normal religious belief but nevertheless says that, if true (and he does not give any argument against it), it demonstrates that God is 'vastly wiser and more powerful than we are'.[49]

For the next few paragraphs let us assume that the Big Bang theory for the origin of the universe is correct.[50] Why are there stars? (Our sun upon which our planet earth depends for all its life is a star.)

If the big bang is a mystery then so is the fine tuning necessary to guarantee that the universe actually produced stars and galaxies so that there could be a planet like earth for us to live on. In the 1960s Sir Bernard Lovell the famous Manchester astronomer calculated that:

> If the rate of expansion had been less by only one part in a thousand billion, then the initial fire ball would have collapsed in on itself before its constituent parts would have been able to form any of the constituents of the stars. There would have been then a universe with no stars (and therefore no sun), no planets - nothing solid or liquid for animals to stand on or fishes to swim in.
>
> If the expansion rate had been a very tiny bit greater, gravitation would not have been able to hold the gases so that stars could not then have formed. Again there would have been nothing solid – everything would just have been gas!

Since Sir Bernard Lovell made that calculation the fine tuning seems even more remarkable. If any of the fundamental forces of nature (such as gravity, electomagnetism and others) had been a tiny bit stronger or weaker then stars and planets like ours could not have existed.

How was our planet earth made?

But even the stars too had to be just of the right kind. Think about our planet, Earth. Where did the chemical elements that make up our water, rocks and soils come from? Remember that the big bang only made hydrogen and helium atoms. There wasn't any iron, oxygen, carbon or anything that is in our planet earth then. So how were these heavier elements formed?

It is generally believed that these elements are the products of huge supernova explosions of the bigger stars. Stars don't burn for ever. The bigger ones end their lives in huge explosions that create these heavier elements and scatter the debris throughout space. From this debris, it is believed, planets like our earth were formed. John Polkinghorne puts it very well:

---

[49]   See his chapter on Leibniz in his *History of Western Philosophy*.

[50]   For doubts about this theory see the open letter (referred to in footnote 26 above) now signed by over 200 scientists originally published in *New Scientist*, May 22, 2004.

. . . stars also have a very important thing to do. The nuclear furnaces that burn inside the stars are the source of the chemical elements which are the raw materials of life . . . For life you need a much more complicated chemistry than hydrogen and helium . . . In particular you need the chemistry of carbon, which [is the basic constituent of] those macro molecules which are the basis of life. To make the carbon you have to make three helium nuclei stick together (a very delicate operation). Then you've got to make lots more elements (oxygen for example). That means another helium atom to stick to the carbon. But be careful, you mustn't overdo it. You mustn't turn all the carbon into oxygen else the carbon will be lost. All these balances must be exactly right until you get up to iron. (The centre of stars cannot make anything beyond iron). Two problems remain: You've got to make heavier elements than iron and you've got to get them all out of the centre of the star so they can become part of the environment of the universe so that planets like earth which contain these elements can be formed. So you must arrange that these stars explode and scatter their elements AND that the explosion itself is of just the right type as to blow off neutrinos to cause the formation of heavier elements such as lead.[51]

These examples give a brief summary of the Fine Tuning of the Universe that make it so exquisite.

One of the world's most distinguished astro-physicists is Paul Davies. He makes no claim to religious belief. Now see what he has to say about the fine tuning of the universe by reading chapter 13 of his book *God and the New Physics*. In this chapter he says that the fine tuning is like firing a gun and hitting a target the size of a postage stamp positioned on the other side of the universe.[52]

Some who want to reject the conclusion that the universe must have had a Designer will respond that any universe might appear fine tuned. To this I further respond that the fine tuning referred to here is that which is necessary to produce any solid existence at all. All the other alternatives would produce gas or black holes only.

Peter Atkins is a well-known militant atheist scientist (chemistry is his subject). His response[53] to the fine-tuning mystery is to say that there may be many other universes and ours just happens to be the one among many billions of universes where initial conditions were just right. If our universe's existence had only depended on one incredible example of fine tuning then it would be

---

[51] This is my selection of some of his points on Fine Tuning in his Hockerill Educational Foundation Lecture 1992.

[52] Davies P., 1984, *God and The New Physics*, p. 179.

[53] In a video produced for school pupils which explains the Universe's Fine Tuning.

possible to argue that case. However the universe's existence requires many exquisitely fine tuned initial conditions all to occur at the same moment. The Oxford mathematician Roger Penrose (who makes no religious profession) has said that expecting to find a universe so fine tuned as ours would be like finding a pencil balanced on its point after an earthquake! In other words, our universe is very improbable indeed.

New evidence for the nature of the fine tuning keeps accumulating. We now know that, in order for a planet to sustain complex life, it needs to be in a very special place in a very special star system in a very special part in a very special galaxy. In addition, it needs to have a right-sized moon (unusually large for our size of planet) and right-positioned gas planets (such as Jupiter), and tectonic plates of the right thickness, to sustain any complex life. Further the universe needs to be as dense at it is (i.e. the size and mass that it is) for a planet like earth to exist at all.

Therefore we can side with Hamlet. He may be exaggerating, but he says:
What a piece of work is man! How noble in reason! how infinite in faculties! in form and moving, how express and admirable! in action, how like an angel! in apprehension, how like a god: the beauty of the world! the paragon of animals! And yet, to me, what is this quintessence of dust?

Even granting for a moment that the incredible fine tuning found in our universe could be explained by saying that our universe may be just one amongst a trillion trillion universes there is much more to the reality of our universe than just an amazing and intricate arrangement of its atoms and forces.

Although the fine tuning of the universe is a recent discovery, philosophers have always been aware that the world seems, at least, to show evidence of design. Their question has been: 'Does that show that there must have been a designer?'

What then have the sceptical philosophers said about this?

One of the greatest of sceptics was David Hume who lived in eighteenth-century Scotland. Sceptical philosophers since him have added little to his basic arguments – they have just rehashed them and attempted to update them. David Hume's most readable (and indeed entertaining) arguments are found in his *Dialogues Concerning Natural Religion*.

Here is a summary of his points that are relevant to this section:

1   He says the universe is bound to have the *appearance* of design.

Any universe would need to have its parts adapted to one another. That is to say, any universe would have to have some order. Since we know any universe would appear to be designed, how do we know that the universe actually is designed?

Here is a quote from the modern philosopher John Hick's book *Philosophy of Religion* – page 29, in which he summarises David Hume's argument:

The fact that there is only one universe precludes our making probable judgements about it. If – impossibly – we knew that there were a number of universes (e.g. 10) and if in addition we knew that (say) half of these were God-produced and half not, then we would deduce that the probability of our own universe being God-produced would be one in two. However, since by the universe we mean the totality of all that is (other than the creator of the universe), clearly no reasoning based on frequency theory of probability is possible concerning its character.

My response is as follows:

The false assumption behind Hume's reasoning is the belief that it is possible to have a non designed universe. In fact, it is not possible. Any universe would appear to be designed because there can be no natural existence without design, whatever form it takes.

I expand a little on that point: the existence of anything means its parts must hold together and relate to one another and they cannot do this unless there are fundamental laws of existence which presuppose order. Any natural existence would appear ordered because any natural existence would be ordered. Another hypothetical universe might have completely different laws of nature than ours but it would still have to have some laws of nature, and therefore would have been designed by a Designer.

2   David Hume rightly says that if the order of nature were created by a Supreme Being, then He must have order in Himself. He then asks, 'If a Supreme Being is capable of non-created order, why should not the world have a non-created order?'

This question is based on what some philosophers call a category mistake. It applies a principle of the finite universe of nature – namely, that effects have causes – to the realm of the eternal supernatural.

The question as to who made something, is a question only applicable to the something if it is part of the natural order. We cannot know from nature what questions are applicable to that which is beyond nature.

We shall consider Bertrand Russell's remaining questions in the next chapter.

Chapter 3
Ethics in Crisis

When everything is moving at once, nothing appears to be moving, as on board ship. When everyone is moving towards depravity, no one seems to be moving, but if someone stops, he shows up the others who are rushing on, by acting as a fixed point.[54]

Russell's last two questions (page 23) can be rephrased as follows:

Does real goodness exist independently of our own opinions – individual or collective? If goodness does exist, how are we to partake in it?

In other words, does the concept of absolute, objective moral values have any validity, or is goodness entirely subjective, just a matter of personal opinion?

According to the latter, subjectivist viewpoint, each individual person or each individual society decides the difference between good and evil, and each opinion is as valid as any other. Thus, there is no goodness independent of human opinions.

According to this view, there is no way to settle a dispute about what is good. There is no point even trying, because the question of who is right has no meaning.

This problem is graphically illustrated in the following hypothetical example: Hitler believed that only some human life is valuable. He ordered the killing of millions of people, believing that humans of their type have no value at all. He felt like it, believed it right, and so did many others. Suppose he had won the war, brainwashed or killed those who disagreed with him, so that the remaining human society came to believe that the holocaust was right, would that have made it right? Or is there some objective goodness – independent of a person or society's beliefs and feelings – that says it is wrong even if every person believes it to be right?

This hypothetical example is not as far-fetched as it might seem. Stephen Pinker (*The Blank Slate*, 2002) writes that 'several scholars have noticed that their students are unequipped to explain why Nazism was wrong, because the students feel it is impermissible to criticize the values of another culture.'

---

[54] Pascal, *Pensées* 699. (I owe this quotation to Thomas V. Morris, *Making Sense of It All*, p. 104.)

Are certain actions intrinsically right or wrong, or are right and wrong merely matters of culture and public opinion?

In 1960, Bertrand Russell wrote:

> I cannot see how to refute arguments for the subjectivity of moral values, but I find myself incapable of believing that all that is wrong with wanton cruelty is that I don't like it.[55]

Commenting on Russell's views, his contemporary philosopher and biographer Alan Wood writes:

> Within Russell's own life time men came to power in great nations who openly challenged old and new moralities. They said Christian ideas were mistaken, that it was right for the strong to kill off the weak, for a Nordic race to exterminate non-Aryans, and for Bolsheviks to enslave non-Bolsheviks. They defended cruelty and falsehood, *and Russell could not prove that they were wrong.* On his principles he could only say 'I dislike your views very much, but I have to admit this is purely a matter of personal opinion'.[56] *[emphasis added]*

In a wide-ranging review of the moral sense and its place in the human personality, Henry Haslam (*The Moral Mind*, 2005) argues that although our moral values are our own, and to that extent subjective, we can only make sense of these subjective values if we recognise the existence of objective values. The more strongly we disagree with another person's moral principles, the more firmly we are acknowledging the existence of true moral values outside ourselves, objective values which we are striving to understand and attain, objective values of which our own subjective values are imperfect reflections.

Evolution and attitudes to life

If we think of our essence as mere accidental descent from bacteria, we can find it depressing, as did George Bernard Shaw. He wrote of Darwinian evolution:

> When its whole significance dawns on you, your heart sinks into a heap of sand within you. There is a hideous fatalism about it, a ghastly and damnable reduction of beauty and intelligence, of strength and purpose, of honour and aspiration.[57]

Or we can rejoice in the meaninglessness of life – and allow the strong to eliminate the weak as in the quote of H. G. Wells who revelled in the ruthlessness of nature: He said:

---

[55] 'Notes on Philosophy', January 1960, Philosophy, 35, pp. 146-47.
[56] Bertrand Russell, *The Passionate Sceptic*, 1957, p. 61.
[57] Quoted by Dawkins in *The Devil's Chaplain*.

And how will the New Republic treat the inferior races? How will it deal with the black? . . . the yellow man? . . . the Jew? . . . those swarms of black, and brown, and dirty-white, and yellow people, who do not come into the new needs of efficiency? Well, the world is a world, and not a charitable institution, and I take it they will have to go . . .

And the ethical system of these men of the New Republic, the ethical system which will dominate the world state, will be shaped primarily to favour the procreation of what is fine and efficient and beautiful in humanity – beautiful and strong bodies, clear and powerful minds . . .

And the method that nature has followed hitherto in the shaping of the world, whereby weakness was prevented from propagating weakness . . . is death . . .

The men of the New Republic . . . will have an ideal that will make the killing worth the while.[58]

Or we can attempt to rise above the meaninglessness of life in the personal existentialism of Sartre and Camus.[59] Or perhaps we can take the post-modern position of the present era, which I refer to again soon.

Sociobiology: An alternative way of understanding human behaviour and morality

The term 'sociobiology' was defined by Edward O Wilson in *Sociobiology: The New Synthesis* as the systematic study of the biological basis of all social behaviour. The study emphasises natural selection as the main factor responsible for our behaviour. Wilson expounds this further in his later book, *Consilience*.[60]

Natural selection has its own values (if it helps survival and breeding it is good; if not, not) and it cannot support any other values. It therefore cannot explain morality, which has its own, different values. Wilson himself wrote on p. 3 of *Sociobiology* that the central theoretical problem of sociobiology was 'how can altruism . . . evolve by natural selection?' The answer he gave was 'kinship'. However, there is much more to morality than the kind of altruism that can be explained by natural selection and the human moral sense cannot be explained by natural selection alone – as argued by Haslam on the basis of his wide review of many different kinds of moral thinking.

Sometimes supporters of sociobiology say we actually exist for the benefit and propagation of our genes:

---

58   Quoted by Dawkins in *The Devil's Chaplain*.
59   For example Sartre, *Nausea* and Camus, *The Outsider*.
60   See my critical review (published in the journal: *Philosophia Christi*). The review is also on my web pages.

We are machines built by DNA whose purpose is to make more copies of the same DNA . . . Flowers are for the same thing as everything else in the living kingdoms, for spreading 'copy me' programmes about, written in DNA language.

This is EXACTLY what we are for. We are machines for propagating DNA, and the propagation of DNA is a self-sustaining process. It is every living object's sole reason for living.[61]

The individual organism is only the vehicle (of genes), part of an elaborate device to preserve and spread them with the least possible biochemical perturbation.. The organism is only DNA's way of making more DNA.[62][63]

There is no way to rationalise a view of the purpose or value of human life, or any life, if one holds these views.

Objectivist Ethics

In opposition to this we have Objectivist Ethics. This is founded on the belief that there is something called goodness which is independent of us – out there somewhere or revealed by God. 'This action is good' means it conforms to that goodness. 'This action is bad' means it is in opposition to that goodness.

Can one derive an 'ought' from an 'is'?

Science can tell us what *is* the case, but can it tell us what *ought* to be the case? Electrons behave as they do – that is neither morally right nor wrong – it is just the way things are – *the whole story*. We behave in certain ways but that is *not the whole story* for we know we ought to behave in certain other ways. Therefore there is more than one kind of reality. The first of these realities is subject to scientific investigation and discovery. The other one isn't – and yet somehow we are convinced that objective moral values exist and are real. However distant they may seem, and however much we may differ from other people about details of morality, we have a sense that these values are there, validating our own moral struggles.

After a period in the twentieth century when subjectivist theories of morality were popular among philosophers, most recent writers support the idea of objective values. Some of these writers are atheists, but attempts to reconcile objective moral values with atheism are not very successful.

---

[61] R Dawkins, 'The Ultraviolet Garden', Royal Institution Christmas Lecture No. 4, 1991.

[62] E O Wilson, *Sociobiology: The New Synthesis*, Harvard University Press, 1975, p. 3.

[63] I owe both these quotations to Denis Alexander's *Rebuilding the Matrix*, p. 274.

Christian Objectivist Ethics

Our moral awareness must be something above and beyond what we actually do. It must be something real that is pressing on us, though we often try to forget it. We, from the inside, know there is a moral imperative. We cannot follow it, but God comes to us and from the inside makes us what we ought to be.

Many people think Christian Ethics is a list of rules found in the Church or the Bible. It is true there are commandments but that is not the *basis* of Christian Ethics. Lists of rules cannot define true Goodness because it is deeply personal. Personal relationships (e.g. friendship) cannot be defined by a list of rules about how we relate to one another. If we are friends with someone and then try to frame rules and obligations to define our friendship, we will fail and spoil the friendship. Hence in the Biblical revelation, God only adds laws because we are already sinners[64] and we live by faith not by works of the law.[65]

Christian goodness means being 'godly' i.e. having the character of Christ in relationships with God, our fellow humans, and the natural world.

This character of God is shown not in rules but in a Person (Jesus Christ). In Christ, God self-sacrificially suffers for our sins giving us forgiveness so as to lift us up to where we belong eternally. That is the meaning of 'love' and it sums up true goodness and greatness.

The cross of Jesus has a better effect on us than 1,000 rules and commandments. By the grace of God we are called to love as He loves us.

This goodness of God shines through all of nature. So all peoples (of whatever culture) intuitively recognise there is something real called 'goodness'. This is so even if they don't know where it has come from.

We often reject that goodness and so have a bad conscience and feel guilty. However Christ's cross brings us forgiveness and new life.

In this imperfect world we need guidance in the form of commandments, so God gives us the Ten Commandments, the Sermon on the Mount and much other teaching.

Indeed, when those who do not have the 'teaching' *[i.e. The Ten Commandments etc.]*, do by nature things required by the 'teaching', they are a law for themselves, even though they do not have the 'teaching', since they show that the requirements of the 'teaching' are written on their hearts, their consciences also bearing witness, and their thoughts now accusing, now even defending them.[66]

---

[64] Galatians 3:19.
[65] Romans 9:32; Galatians 2:16.
[66] Romans 2:14-15.

Modernism and Postmodernism

First, what does the term **Modernism** mean?

It has taken many differing forms, mainly expressing beliefs about science and/or politics and the meaning of human history. It has taken the quest for certainty without reference to religion. Modernism that puts all its faith in science (naturalism is this kind of modernism) usually holds that objective scientific method can be applied across the board in the soft sciences such as sociology and psychology. Since the physical sciences cannot tell us what ought to be the case, only what is the case, it finds it difficult to place morality in its scheme. A scientific approach, such as that attempted by Henry Haslam[67] can observe and record the moral sentiments that people hold, and it can see how the moral sense engages with different aspects of the human personality, but it cannot make a moral judgement about the relative merits of different moral principles.

Naturalistic explanations of how our moral sense developed may or may not be valid. But that is not the point. The real question is whether or not our moral sense is sensing anything real – something non-physical that is pressing upon us, telling us what we ought to be doing. Haslam concludes from his survey that the (subjective) moral sentiments in the human personality only make sense if objective values exist: the most reasonable interpretation of the scientific evidence is that such values are real, although this cannot be proved by scientific means. Haslam also comments on the reluctance of mainstream psychology to recognise the moral sense as an important part of the human personality. As an example, he observes that *The Oxford Companion to the Mind* has no articles on conscience, ethics, guilt, morality, temptation or values. But how can one understand human mind without considering these concepts? Haslam goes on to comment about mainstream psychologists: 'Ethics has a place in their own practical workaday lives, but, as theorists, they construct a model of the human personality in which ethical considerations have no part.'

I am reminded of those professionals who advocate mere physical forces to explain different aspects of humanity's behaviour, beliefs and thoughts. They always make the exception of themselves! They assume that their own lectures, TV programs, and books were not composed as a result of the previous distribution of particles in the universe, but as a result of their own reasoning that was free to make moral judgements and pronouncements as to how they

---

[67] *The Moral Mind*, 2005 Imprint Academic.

believe society (say) should act towards all the other people who can't help do what they do and believe what they believe.

In August 1999 I went to Cornwall to see the total eclipse of the sun. Astronomers using mathematics had correctly predicted this event many decades before. We can understand the behaviour of the stars and our moon by scientific laws. Modernism usually holds that all events in the universe (including my thoughts and efforts to write this book) could be predicted in much the same sort of way. Laplace, the early nineteenth-century French scientist whose views were similar to those of the modern-day naturalists, wrote:

> An intelligence that knew at one moment of time all the forces by which nature is animated and the respective positions of the entities which compose it, would embrace in the same formula the movements of the largest bodies in the universe and those of the lightest atoms; nothing would be uncertain for it, and the future, like the past, would be present to its eyes.

If this were true then it would have been possible, hundreds of years before the event, to predict the writing of Beethoven's Ninth Symphony. So, in principle, from this prediction it would have been possible to actually write the music before Beethoven. But then it would have been possible to predict the prediction and so on back to the beginning of the world and beyond perhaps! There must be more to Beethoven's genius than scientifically analysable physical particles, laws and forces. Again, naturalism fails.

Others, holding to modernism, thought they could derive certainty from history and politics. Marxism was one political example of modernism. It held that certain economic, class and political laws could be applied to human history giving certainty as to its direction which would lead to a utopian communism.

Problems with Modernism

Political theories broke down. Marxism simply proved itself wrong.

Instead of science solving all mysteries, its advance revealed, and continues to reveal, more and more mysteries undreamed of by an earlier generation. So it was seen that it couldn't answer the ultimate questions after all.

And then there is the perceived harmful influence of modernism giving us wars, pollution etc. There is also its perceived depersonalising tendencies, not being able to come to terms with our personal self-awareness and spiritual longings. Its optimistic belief in progress has been undermined by recent human history.

So if the Meta-narratives (the big stories or worldviews that attempt to explain the world) of Modernism fail should we return to the big stories or Meta-narratives of religion? Postmodernism says No!

Jean-Francois Lyotard (French Canadian), in 1979, defined Postmodernism as 'incredulity towards (all) Meta-narratives'. Neither science nor politics nor religion gives us universal truth. There is no 'big story' – there is no universal truth. However don't worry – just pick and mix what makes you feel good. Don't consider the big questions. Just enjoy your own little world. Mix together ancient and modern images, sayings and teachings. Don't ask yourself what they mean – meaning does not matter – there is no universal meaning. If possible enjoy both religious services and speeches by atheists. If they appear to contradict one another – don't worry – its how they make you feel that matters. Just don't get bored.

Postmodernism is a 'care-free' attitude to life, coming from the conviction that there are no universal truths.

If there are no truths then there can be no moral judgement that this behaviour, custom, music or art is better than that behaviour, custom, music or art. In one of my 'Philosophy of Science and Theology' Adult Education classes in a UK university I gave the students (adults) two statements and asked for their comments.

1 Water Boils at 100^0 C at sea level *whatever the local culture says*.

One student disagreed. She held that cultures decide 'truth' – i.e. truth is subjective not objective.

2 It is morally wrong to kill new-born babies just because they are twins, *whatever the local culture says*.

Three disagreed. Their Teacher Training Colleges and Sociology classes had taught them that cultures must make their own morality – i.e. morality is subjective not objective.

But can the postmodern conviction remain care-free? In a peaceful prosperous environment when life is running smoothly maybe it can. But when troubles and tragedies abound?

So modernism depersonalises us and postmodernism stops us making judgements about right/wrong and beautiful/ugly.

Mary Warnock writes about the prevailing cynicism in our society, which may have a creeping and insidious effect, and especially so in schools, where teachers may find themselves bewildered by their own half-articulate principles that they must not be dogmatic, they must not presume that there are any disinterested or unbiased arguments, and above all they must not be 'judgmental'.[68]

---

[68] *An Intelligent Person's Guide to Ethics*, Duckworth, London 1998.

So how can children be taught the difference between right and wrong and how will they learn to appreciate real beauty and differentiate it from sheer ugliness?

Our society seems to be dominated by the contradictory beliefs of modernism and postmodernism at the same time. A book discussing the appalling results of this in our society is *After Progress* by the President of the Royal Institute of Philosophy, Professor Anthony O'Hear.

However, postmodernism has a major intellectual difficulty. 'There is no absolute truth' is itself a statement that claims to be absolutely true! Postmodernism therefore refutes itself and, like naturalism and modernism, cannot be true!

Is there a reasonable alternative to these views of secularists? I believe there is, and it is Christianity with its roots in the Judaism of the Hebrew scriptures. But even if we accept this, will it give us a sure guide? Well, yes and no. It tells us of an objective reality – the source and meaning of the natural world and all goodness. However it deliberately leaves room for human free will and discussion.

Lord Hailsham:

> It is the objective validity of morality as proclaimed by the sages of all nations which explains and justifies the perpetual tension, the endless dialogue, between individuals and minorities on the one hand and the State on the other, between freedom and authority, between liberty and law. In other words it is the free will and the rationality of the individual, the dignity of the individual, in tension with moral responsibility of the individual which explains and justifies the writings of the political authors, the debates in Parliament, the regulations made by Ministers, the treaties concluded between sovereign communities, the demand for freedom, and the necessity for law which constitute the history of the West, and ultimately of all mankind. The fact that these things are not measurable, calculable, or verifiable explains much, perhaps all, of the argument. But the fact that they remain objective realities proves that the argument is not about nothing. A law which does not appeal to the rational in man is no better than a stick or a carrot applied to a donkey, by whomsoever or whatsoever it is passed.[69]

So we will go on to explore some reasons for believing that the claim that we should turn to the Bible is reasonable.

But first the case against the Church written so eloquently by our erstwhile ally in this book, Lord Hailsham:

---

[69] *The Door Wherein I Went*, p. 64.

At first sight, the history of the Christian Church is not a matter of edification. At the most favourable level, the divine light of the Gospels and the epistles seems to have given place in a matter of a generation or two on the one hand to endless squabbles about unverifiable points of doctrine which continue to divide Christians to this day, and on the other to a mass of pious fables and superstitions, bogus miracles and fake relics, all or most commercially exploited, which have persisted almost continuously from sub-apostolic times, to the bon-dieuserie of shops and shrines which can still be seen all over the Christian world. But this is the least part of it. The cruelties and persecutions, the civil wars and blind hatreds, the autos da fe, the burnings and rackings, the hangings, the drawings and quarterings, the anathemas, the inquisitions, the pogroms, the crusades, the sackings, the holy wars, are not, one would think, good advertisements for the divine society, inspired by the Holy Spirit, against whom we are expressly told the gates of hell shall not prevail, that it is to guard the keys, that its judgements are to be endorsed by the heavenly courts . . . and even if one forgets all this, the amount of sheer and self-contradictory nonsense which emerges from clergy and ecclesiastically-minded laymen on the radio and television when they talk about secular and political subjects is enough to damp the ardour of the most spiritually-minded of devotees. It is not enough to say that the same can be said of the history of most other organised bodies of human beings whether secular or religious, Jews, Moslems, Hindus, Buddhists, Communists, Fascists, and so on. The Church claims to be something special, and it is not enough for it to excuse its appalling record by saying that it shares human faults with other human organisations. It is there to redeem humanity and not to share its failings.[70]

Remembering this is a quotation from his book, which describes how he turned from atheism to Christianity, let us remind ourselves of his words quoted at the beginning of this book. It comes from a much fuller passage as follows:

It remains true, in my experience at least, of the events of my lifetime that the moment a society consciously begins to reject Christianity and its values and, for whatever reason, begins pursuing the opposite, the most startlingly evil practices appear once more to emerge from dark corners and flap their hideous wings abroad. How much of what is now taken for granted in what is good in society owes its original inspiration to a consciously Christian motivation, even where the work has been subsequently overtaken, and taken over, by the apparatus of the modern state. Wilberforce was motivated by Christianity when he set about his campaign to end the slave trade. Florence Nightingale's original motivation was Christian, and the source of her expertise when she first sought to revive the almost forgotten craft of nursing was a teaching order of nuns where the art had

---

[70] *The Door Wherein I Went*, p. 43.

been kept alive. Our whole system of education, public and private, our network of hospitals, our social security system itself, have each a clear origin in Christian foundations and, whatever can be said against much of the theorisation, and much of the practice which they embodied, the motivation which underlay them was good and, in origin at least, the practice was disinterested. The Christians have been pioneers of good work throughout their history. They have been the originators, and secular society has largely caught up with their efforts, made good their deficiencies of scale, and corrected their faults. No one who has studied the ancient world can get very far without being horror-struck with the hurricane of libido, lust, cruelty and greed of which Jung spoke, and those of us who have an increasing contact with the post-Christian society in which we live are disturbed to find the very same features reproducing themselves under widely differing political systems, in almost exact proportions as the spirit ceases to be cultivated, and the life of the spirit lived.[71]

How do we reconcile these passages? The first is about the history of a Christian Church where spiritual authority is misused. The second is about Christianity as revealed in the Bible. What does he say about the Bible itself?

Looking back on my life I find that the Bible in its coherent entirety has been one of the main influences on my character and conduct. I believe this is true of everyone who has come into contact with it and has not deliberately chosen to disregard its message. It is impossible to read the Bible out loud week after week without finding the immense power and vitality of almost every part of it. It seems to come to life and movement on your lips like a living thing. It almost wriggles, like a fish on the line, like a snake in the hand. It is not a dead word, but a living word . . . It is when it is treated as a living source of inspiration and enlightenment that it does its work. It can only be used in conjunction with the life of meditation, self-criticism and prayer. But so used there is nothing like it, and there is no substitute for it.[72]

I add here that if one wants to find a book that is as clear as any in its denunciation of the exploitation of spiritual power and abuse of spiritual teachings (albeit God given spiritual authority and teaching), there is none better than the Bible itself.[73]

The world does not need more religion – it has plenty already. But it does need God as revealed in Christ, who loved his enemies, prayed for those who persecuted Him, suffered human death to take away the sins of the world and reconcile us to Himself.

---

[71] *The Door Wherein I Went*, p. 48.
[72] *The Door Wherein I Went*, p. 71.
[73] For example: Matthew 23.

Rather than leading an army and killing people, He suffered for the sins of the world although he had done no violence, nor was any deceit in his mouth.[74] In His resurrection from the dead, He promised to come again in power to judge the world in righteousness and save those who humbly look to Him.

If He had promised us a perfect Church or a permanently strong Church then we would have reason to lose faith in His word. On the contrary Jesus tells us:

Not everyone who says to me, 'Lord, Lord,' will enter the kingdom of heaven, but only he who does the will of my Father who is in heaven. Many will say to me on that day, 'Lord, Lord, did we not prophesy in your name, and in your name drive out demons and perform many miracles?' Then I will tell them plainly, 'I never knew you. Away from me, you evildoers!' [75]

So we must go on to think about the trustworthiness of the Bible itself.

Chapter 4
Why The Bible's Revelation Is Trustworthy

Much in this chapter, after the sub heading beginning: 'The Nature and Origin of the Bible', was first published by Christian Focus as a Chapter in their book *Serving the Word of God*. It was a tribute to Revd James Philip on his 80th birthday.

The naturalist worldview can be summarised rather like this:

- In the beginning there were particles and impersonal laws of physics.
- Somehow they got together and formed living stuff.
- The stuff imagined God.
- And then discovered evolution.[76]

This contrasts with the Biblical alternative:

In the beginning was the Word, and the Word was with God, and the Word was God. He was in the beginning with God.

All things were made through him, and without him was not any thing made that was made.

And the Word became flesh and dwelt among us, and we have seen his glory, glory as of the only Son from the Father, full of grace and truth.[77]

---

[74] Isaiah 53:9 (NIV) These prophetic words from the Hebrew Scriptures show us what is at the centre of the vision of righteousness which Jesus lived and taught.
[75] Matt 7:21-23 (NIV).
[76] I owe this to Philip Johnson's *The Right Questions*.
[77] John 1:1-3,14.

It was the two beliefs enshrined in these words of John that gave experimental science its lift off. These are (1) nature has a rational structure open to the human mind and (2) its rational structure did not have to be as it is by logical necessity, but rather was chosen to be this way and not that way. Thus to understand nature we have to examine it. It was important that the Bible itself influenced society, rather than the often-misused authority of ecclesiastical figures.

So how is mind known? I can only know your mind by hearing you speak or communicate in words. If I with reason believe what you say, that is have faith in you, I trust that your words express your mind. By examining your brain I could never discover your thoughts – your mind. I need to hear your 'word'. In that personal relationship with you, listening to what you say, I can learn something of your mind. Again, the Bible puts it like this:

> For who among men knows the thoughts of a man except the man's spirit within him? In the same way no one knows the thoughts of God except the Spirit of God.
>
> The man without the Spirit does not accept the things that come from the Spirit of God, for they are foolishness to him, and he cannot understand them, because they are spiritually discerned. 'For who has known the mind of the Lord that he may instruct him?' But we have the mind of Christ.[78]

Surely that which lies behind the existence of all things cannot be less than us. We are personal beings who (however imperfectly) know something of the meaning of love. He (we dare no longer say 'it') must be at least personal and very great love.

Love is self-giving – even to the undeserving.

Not only is the existence of God necessary to make sense of the grandeur and beauty of reality but so also is the Cross of Christ in whom He makes Himself known in the midst of the suffering, ugliness and evil of the world. This leads us to consider the nature and origin of the Bible.

The Nature and Origin of the Bible

The Bible tells us that the Word of God is established eternally in heaven.[79] However it is not the Christian claim that the Bible itself has existed eternally in heaven, or that the Bible will be needed once God's people leave this world and go to heaven. This contrasts with the Muslim claim about their book the

---

[78] 1 Corinthians 2:11-16.
[79] Psalm 119:89.

Qur'an. Muslims believe that, although it was only finally revealed on earth through Mohammed approximately 1300 years ago, the Qur'an is a transcript of a tablet preserved in heaven eternally with God.

The New Testament makes clear what is implicit in the Old Testament, namely that the Eternal Word is not a 'thing' (a book) but the very personal expression (Word) of the mind of God who sustains all creation and works out the plan of salvation for the world.[80] In the New Testament the eternal and personal Mind or Word came among us clothed in our full humanity so that we might know Him face to face.[81] The Bible is both the account of, and the result of, this very real and personal engagement of God's eternal mind with the history of the world. Through this very personal self-disclosure by God the Bible was written. Unless we use the Bible to receive knowledge of the Eternal Word we will never really understand it.

Here is an interesting comment about the Bible from a learned Hindu.

I can't understand why you missionaries present the Bible to us in India as a book of religion. It is not a book of religion – and anyway we have plenty of books of religion in India. We don't need any more! I find in your Bible a unique interpretation of universal history, the history of the whole of creation and the history of the human race. And therefore a unique interpretation of the human person as a responsible actor in history. That is unique. There is nothing else in the whole religious literature of the world to put alongside it.[82]

So then the Bible claims to be the book that is the record of God's very personal revelation of Himself to humankind so that we might know Him who is our Creator, Lord and Judge, and so discover His salvation for our lost humanity and spoilt world.

How can we understand and assess this claim? How should we study it?

I use an example from another branch of knowledge – astronomy. (Examples could be taken from any number of branches of knowledge.)

The world's great telescopes are amazing instruments full of all kinds of gadgets to enable the astronomer to come to a knowledge of the particular part of the heavens he is viewing. Let us imagine a team of technicians coming to examine this instrument and make sense of it, without realising that its purpose is to view distant objects in the skies beyond it. They will all try to work out what this and that gadget is for, and write many learned papers about

---

[80]   John 1:1-2.
[81]   John 1:14-18.
[82]   This quotation is taken from Lesslie Newbigin, *A Walk Through the Bible*.

them. If they are writing independently of one another they will all have different ideas about which parts of the instrument are useful and which are useless, which were original and which were later additions, which are fundamental and which are merely superficial.

What is certain is that they will never be able to make sense of it as a whole until they discover what it is for, and they won't find that until they actually look through it. Once they have made this fundamental discovery then they will gradually be able to make sense of the whole. As they actually use the telescope for its purpose of viewing reality beyond it in the heavens then it will, as it were, be able to unfold its many and varied recourses to them and they will see it as a wonderful inter-related unity. If they refuse to take into account the purpose of the telescope in their investigations, we would have to say that the whole basis of their work is irrational even though it has the appearance of being scientific.

Similarly our understanding of the Bible can only come when we use it for its purpose, which is to lead us to personal knowledge of God. If we resist such life-changing knowledge we will never be able to assess the truth of the Bible. We cannot be detached observers or listeners.

The Bible is the account of the relationship of God with all creation. Although the Bible writings were all complete by the first century AD, its story, in both Old and New Testaments, looks ahead to the end of time. Its story begins at the beginning of creation and finishes in the future at the close of the present age. The Bible therefore encompasses the whole of reality and does not allow us the dualist way of thinking that would seek to break up knowledge into disconnected parts. It cannot be considered as if it were just a religious book divorced from such subjects as history or science. More of this later.

The Bible is dominated by the figure of the Almighty and living God who creates, redeems and judges according to His own loving and righteous purposes which come from the heart of His being. In the pages of the Bible we come face to face with Him as He speaks, calls and expects a response.[83] God is therefore revealed in the Scriptures as deeply personal and something must be said here about personal knowledge.

Personal knowledge of one another is not gained primarily through looking at one another but through listening to one another. It is through speech that we reveal what is really on our heart and mind. Thus God's revelation of Himself is in terms of 'Word' rather than picture. We must not seek to make any image of Him. Because knowledge of Him must be based on personal relationship,

---

[83] I owe some of the wording of this paragraph to Lesslie Newbigin.

knowledge of Him is not primarily knowledge of a philosophical principle or ground of being. Also it is not primarily knowledge of certain codes or laws. We know Him as a Person as we know all persons. Personal knowledge always has trust and love at its heart, and therefore a willingness to receive, give and be changed by our growth in understanding of other persons.

Because God is Person, it belongs to the heart of the message of the Bible that our response to Him must be faith and obedience rather than human wisdom or works of the law. Philosophical discussions, words of wisdom and codes of law do find their essential place in the Bible, but only as servants of that true knowledge of God that comes through faith.

This means that we should not seek to discover truth by extracting doctrines from the text of Scripture and then merely comparing them with one another. That would lead to the detaching doctrine from the deeply personal knowledge that is appropriate for God. The doctrines that we find in our Bible study must only be considered in relation to that profoundly personal knowledge of God that is revealed in His personal relationship with His people. Indeed it is common to hear conversion testimonies from men and women who say that they once found the Bible meaningless but when they experienced openness to God himself, the Bible came alive.

The Bible claims to be about the relationship between God and all of His creation. However it is primarily concerned with His relationship with human beings for we are created to be the link between the natural world and heaven itself - between God and the rest of creation. Further, it is we who have sinned against Him, bringing suffering to the world. Hence the story of redemption as told in the Bible particularly concerns God and humankind.

Because the nations and peoples are many, God chose one people, to represent all peoples, who would be the human bearers of God's purposes in redemption. They, the chosen people, were given a land – the Promised Land – in which God would work out His purpose for the world.

Because they were uniquely to be the ones who would receive the Divine Word, God's deeply personal relationship with humankind became particularly intense in His relation with the Jewish people (Israel). They, like the rest of us, were and are sinners. Hence the special intensity of God's relationship with them drew out of them the best and the worst that we see in the human race. Both God's special relationship with them and their inevitably intense response to that relationship ensured that their history would be unique among the nations. Further, their encounter with other nations brought and brings the Gentiles into contact with God's revelation. Therefore the nations' reaction to the Jewish People reveals both the best and the worst, not only in the Jews, but also in the wider world as well. (This is the deepest way to understand the historic and ever-present phenomenon of anti-Semitism.)[84]

In the story of Israel we see, as if in a magnifying mirror, the story of all peoples and the story of our individual lives. That is why the Bible speaks to peoples and individuals of all ages. In it we hear God's Word to us all.

When we reach the New Testament we find that God has not just *drawn near* to Israel, but His Word has actually come *into their midst*. 'The Word became flesh and dwelt among us'.[85] Now the particularly intense relationship that draws out of them both the best and the worst reaches its dramatic climax. It is in this climax that God is able fully to reveal His Person to us. It is at the Cross that God's heart of love and righteousness is fully made known. This final revelation is foreshadowed in all His past relationship with Israel as recorded in the Old Testament. Thus the whole Old Testament bears witness to Christ,[86] not just a few passages. In Him the full relationship between God and humankind, foreshadowed in the Old Testament, is finally revealed. That is why the New Testament draws upon Old Testament words spoken to Israel and applies them to Jesus. Since Israel embodies before God, all peoples, it also is right for preachers to use such passages and relate them to the wider world, church and individuals.

It is in the culmination of meeting between God and Israel that the worst and best about His people is finally seen. The best is seen, for example, in the life of the Apostles (all Jews) who accept Christ, and begin to take the Word of God into all the world, thus fulfilling God's calling to Israel to be a light to the Gentiles.

The worst is seen in the Jewish religious leadership who reject Christ and in doing so reject the very Person of God Himself. Yet it is here that we see the wonderful sovereign love of God for us all. Not only does God use their good response to Christ, He needs and uses also their rejection of Him too. Indeed their rejection of Him is the means by which He fully makes Himself known to us as He bears all our sins in His body and *'takes away the sins of the world'*.[87]

Both Old and New Testament, tell us that God had actually purposed to use the sin of Israel as the means of bringing light to the world.[88] His righteous love is seen in the context of the sin of His people. Although the cross of Christ is the place where this is accomplished, it is seen too in the Old Testament. Here also the wonderful love and forgiveness of God are demonstrated in the

---

[84] See Psalm 44:15-22.

[85] John 1:14.

[86] Luke 24:44.

[87] John 1:29.

[88] Isaiah 42:18-19, Romans 11 (whole chapter).

context of the sin of Israel. It is only in that context that such books as Jeremiah could have been written at all.[89] This is a major theme of Paul's epistle to the Romans. Here he argues that it is human unfaithfulness to God that brings out His faithfulness and that is the way He had purposed it from the beginning. [90]

It is out of this very real and dramatic relationship between God and Israel that Old and New Testaments came to be written. The writings of the Scriptures are the response to all that has happened as the life of God meets the people of Israel. The Bible is the result of the Divine really embedding itself in the humanity of God's people. Those who were most intimately caught up in the drama record that Divine initiative and human response for us. They were not detached observers.

Thus the writing of the Bible can be considered both from the perspective of the Divine and from that of humans. However, it must never be forgotten that its ultimate origin is God, not man. It is not that part of it is divine and part human. It is entirely divine and entirely human. It is in the very human words of the Biblical writers that the divine Word is heard in all its fullness. The bond between the Divine and the human is always the Holy Spirit. That is why the human authors of the Bible, writing with all their varying degrees of good or bad Hebrew or Greek, nevertheless through the inspiration of the Holy Spirit, really are enabled to bring the Word of God to the world. That is what the Bible is.

God raises Christ, having died as a Jew at the hand of Jews and Gentiles in a new recreated humanity that breaks the human division between Jew and Gentile. In the resurrection of Christ, Israel is reconstituted and the Church that embraces both Jew and Gentile becomes, through Christ, the new Temple. This is a major point made by Paul in Ephesians.[91]

In Romans 11, Paul goes on to discuss the future for both the Church and Jewish Israel. He argues that it is precisely because God had purposed that Jewish Israel be disobedient for our sake that He has not abandoned the purposes for them that are revealed in the Old Testament prophets. *Thus the Bible tells us about the future destiny of the Church, Jewish Israel and the world.* It is not three separate purposes, though. Rather, through the final restoration of Israel to its land and eventually to Christ, the Church itself will be blessed and, in turn, the world experience *'life from the dead'.*[92] (This does not mean that all will be saved, for although the resurrection of Christ embraces all creation there are many, both

---

89 See for example Jeremiah 30 and 31.
90 Romans 3:1-6.
91 Ephesians 2:14ff.
92 Romans 11:15.

Jew and Gentile, who reject the grace of God. This means there will be both a resurrection to Eternal Life and a resurrection to condemnation.[93])

Paul also makes clear that the Christian Church should never look down upon the continuing Jewish Israel, because the very sins of self-righteous pride that led them to reject Christ are in danger of affecting the Church too. Indeed he goes on to imply that if the Church does not live up to its calling it will not succeed in its calling to lead the Jewish people to Christ.[94]

Thus although the Bible story is focused in Israel and then Christ, its story enfolds the whole of reality from the beginning to the end of time.

But now to this question: Is there any external indication that the story it tells is a true story – a true history?

We ponder briefly the human subject of the story – the people of Israel.

As said in an earlier chapter, over again the Old Testament prophets tell us that the history of the Jews will be unlike the history of any other people, and that towards the end of time, after great suffering, the Jews will return to the Promised Land, where they will become the centre of hostility. This hostility will affect the whole world. Eventually God will reconcile them to their Messiah, cleanse them from their sin, judge the nations who have hated them, and make them a blessing to all peoples.[95] The New Testament is not silent about this purpose of God.[96]

Many people find this subject embarrassing because they have been led to believe that Israel today is guilty of oppressing the Palestinians and furthermore the Christian revelation teaches that God loves all peoples – not just the Jews.. To address these concerns I will go over some basic issues.

---

[93] John 5:28-29.

[94] Romans 11:17-24.

[95] Isaiah 43.49; Jer 30 – 33; Ezek 36 – 39; Zech 12 & 13, etc.

[96] For example in Luke 21:20-24 we read: 'When you see Jerusalem being surrounded by armies, you will know that its desolation is near. Then let those who are in Judea flee to the mountains and let those in the city get out . . . for this is the time of punishment in fulfilment of all that has been written . . . They will fall by the sword and be taken as prisoners to all nations. Jerusalem will be trampled on by the Gentiles until the times of the Gentiles are fulfilled.' This passage tells us that the coming scattering of Israel is the true fulfilment of the Old Testament prophecies. We therefore conclude that these Old Testament prophecies cannot have referred only to the Babylonian exile hundreds of years before Christ! That means that the Old Testament prophecies about the restoration after exile must also refer to events after Christ as well as events before His time on earth. This is confirmed by the last words in the above quote which show us that the coming Jewish exile from Jerusalem is not for ever.

Modern Political Considerations.

Many people find it difficult to believe that God's hand is in the restoration of Israel because we are led to believe that they have unjustly displaced Arabs from their land. To respond to this one cannot avoid politics, so I make the following brief points:

1　The Middle East conflict is not just between Israel and the Palestinians but has always been between Israel and the vast Muslim world (i.e. before there was a problem of 'occupied territories' or refugees).

2　The majority of Israeli Jews were, in 1948, of Middle Eastern – not European – descent. It is not true that the majority of Israelis were European Jews running from Nazi ideology. The majority were fleeing Arab persecution they were experiencing in their Arab homelands.

3　Arab Nationalism and the PLO have always claimed that the Palestinians belong to the one 'Arab Nation' that covers the whole Middle East. (See the PLO Covenant). The Arabs have 20 states of their own.　It is absurd then to claim that the Jews are to blame for the fact that the Palestinians have no homeland. All the Jews have ever wanted is just one little one for themselves. (Most Arab nations remain violently hostile to Israel's very existence).

4　The so-called 'occupied territories' never belonged to Palestinians. The West Bank belonged to Jordan and Gaza belonged to Egypt. In 1967 Egypt made blood curdling threats against all Jews and brought its army to the border of Israel and also Jordan attacked Israel. Technically Israel fired the first shot in its war against those who openly said they would destroy Israel. After the end of this war Israel offered to give back the territories in return for peace. At a summit the Arab nations said, 'No peace with Israel, no negotiations with Israel and no recognition of Israel.' So the Israelis kept hold of the territories partly for ideological reasons and partly for security reasons. They began to build settlements on the territories to strengthen their hold.

5　The Arab nations are much larger than even the USA and have long-term oil supplies.　Israel is as small as one of the small states of America. It is about the size of Wales and has had no oil.

6　The cause of the Palestinian refugee problem was war.　The wars were started by the vast and wealthy Arab nations with the sole intention of wiping Israel off the map.　During these wars Arabs (the ones now called Palestinians) suffered at Israeli hands but it was the Arab nations which initiated the wars. This includes the 2009 Gaza conflict which cost so many precious lives which included children.

7   There is no other nation in world history that has survived such overwhelming danger and hatred as Israel today.   Even though they may react violently and unjustly towards the Arab rioters in their midst, I doubt whether any other nation would act with more restraint, given only a fraction of the danger to its very existence.   (If it were to withdraw to its pre-1967 boundaries it would be only nine miles wide at its middle populated area).

8   Although God may indeed judge unjust Israeli actions, other nations will have to face similar judgement for far greater injustices committed with much less excuse.   (One has only to consider Israel's neighbours to realise this, never mind much of the rest of the world.)

Theological Assumptions which colour Christian attitudes against the continuing purposes of God for Israel.

1   If one believes that God's relationship with his creation is purely spiritual (ie He does not interact with the physical space-time of this world) then one will find it difficult to believe that He is active in history so as to give the Jews a unique history among the nations – a history which now has resulted in their regathering. If one does hold this view (a form of Deism) one must still come to terms with the widely recognised fact that Jewish history is remarkable indeed.

If on the other hand one believes that God can and does act in the space-time of this world then will not have a theological problem with the uniqueness of Jewish history and perhaps its restoration to the land.

2   If one believes that the Old Testament is concerned with a particular people and land and not with all the world, and that the New Testament gives this a universal application then one will find it difficult to see how God could have any *continuing special* purpose for Israel and its land. If however one believes that both Old and New Testaments hold particular and universal together (this is the argument of Paul in Romans 2 – 3 and 9 – 11) then one will find it easier to see the continuing significance of land.

3   If one holds the view based on such texts as 1 Peter 2:9, that the mission of ancient Israel has been transferred to the Church (this is called Replacement Theology or Supercessionism), then one will call the Church the new Israel and one will not hold that modern Israel has a unique significance in the purposes of God. This is precisely the kind of conclusion that the Apostle Paul refuses to draw at the end of Romans 2 and the beginning of Romans 3, when discussing the relationship between the new circumcision and the old. If on the other hand we hold that the privileges of ancient Israel are not transferred but used merely to describe the Church, then we will not have any difficulty in recognising the continuing significance of the history of the Jewish people.

4   If one believes that the salvation of Christ is only for the spiritual part of human beings then one will find it difficult to believe that land is significant. If one believes, however, that the redemption of Christ embraces all creation then one will be able to see that land is significant. Since Paul (Rom 9-11) re-affirms God's ancient covenant with Jewish Israel *and that at the heart of this ancient covenant is 'land' one will see why Paul does not need explicitly to refer to their restoration to the land – especially as, at that time, they were not even in exile from the land.*

5   If one believes that Christ fulfils Israel's unique destiny and that 'fulfils' includes in its meaning a 'putting an end to' then one will find it difficult to see the continuing relevance of Israel in the story of redemption. If, however, one believes that Christ fulfils Israel's destiny from Abraham *to the end of time* then one will see Israel's continuing history as 'in Christ' – even if Israel itself does not recognise it.

Jews, Christians, and agnostics have written about the Jewish story and commented on its uniqueness. The ordinary Jewish person is just that. There really is no difference between the Jewish person and the great variety of people one would find in any community. But the history of the Jewish people as a whole is striking in its uniqueness. I give below a few examples.

The following quotes illustrate this uniqueness and some of them come from both web sites belonging to Christians and others belonging to Jewish people.[97]

Winston Churchill:

Some people like the Jews, and some do not. But no thoughtful man can deny the fact that they are, beyond any question, the most formidable and the most remarkable race which has appeared in the world.

Olive Schreiner:[98]

The study of the history of Europe during the past centuries teaches us one uniform lesson: that the nations which received and in any way dealt fairly and mercifully with the Jew have prospered; and that the nations that have tortured and oppressed him have written out their own curse.

---

[97]   For example: http://www.israpundit.com/2006/?p=3633 http://www.shalomdelaware.org/page.aspx?id=182848
http://newsgroups.derkeiler.com/Archive/Soc/soc.culture.polish/2007-06/msg03958.html

[98]   Olive Shreiner was a South African author, pacifist and political activist. She is best known for her novel *The Story of an African Farm*, which has been acclaimed for the manner it tackled the issues of its day, ranging from agnosticism to the treatment of women.

David Vital:[99]

By the standards of others, once they had lost their country, the Jewish people should have fallen into decay long ago. But instead, **uniquely** *[emphasis mine]*, they continued to maintain themselves as a nation, and by doing so became in the eyes of others an uncanny and frightening people.[100]

Mark Twain:

The Jews constitute a tiny percentage of the human race. Properly the Jew ought hardly to be heard of; but he is heard of, has always been heard of. He is as prominent on the planet as any other people, and his commercial importance is extravagantly out of proportion to the smallness of his bulk. His contributions to the world's list of great names in literature, science, art music, finance, medicine and abstruse learning are also way out of proportion to the weakness of his numbers. He has made a marvellous fight in this world, in all the ages; and has done it with has hands tied behind him. He could be vain of himself, and be excused for it. The Egyptian, the Babylon and the Persian rose, filled the planet with sound and splendour, then faded to dream-stuff and passed away; the Greek and the Roman followed, and made a vast noise, and they are gone; other peoples have sprung up and held their torch high for a time, but it burned out, and they sit in twilight now, or have vanished. The Jew saw them all, beat them all, and is now what he always was, exhibiting no decadence, no infirmities of age, no weakening of his parts, no slowing of his energies, no dulling of his alert and aggressive mind. All things are mortal but the Jew; all other forces pass, but he remains. What is the secret of his immortality? [101]

The once Marxist Russian **Nikolai Berdayev**[102] came to a similar conclusion:

I remember how the materialist interpretation of history, when I attempted in my youth to verify it by applying it to the destinies of peoples, broke down in the case of the Jews, where destiny seemed absolutely inexplicable from the materialistic standpoint . . . their survival is a mysterious and wonderful phenomenon demonstrating that the life of this people is governed by a special predetermination, transcending the processes of adaptation expounded by the materialistic interpretation of history. The survival of the Jews, their

---

[99] *David Vital* is Emeritus Nahum Goldmann Professor of Diplomacy at the University of Tel Aviv.

[100] David Vital, *The Origins of Zionism*.

[101] In an essay entitled 'Concerning the Jews' quoted by Lance Lambert in his book, *The Uniqueness of Israel*, p. 57.

[102] Nikolai Alexandrovich Berdyaev was a Russian religious and political philosopher who lived at the end of the 19th century and the beginning of the 20th.

resistance to destruction, their endurance under absolutely peculiar conditions and the fateful role played by them in history: all these point to the particular and mysterious foundations of their destiny.

The historian **Barbara Tuchman**[103] wrote:

The history of the Jews is . . . intensely peculiar in the fact of having given the western world its concept of origins and monotheism, its ethical traditions, and the founder of its prevailing religion, yet suffering dispersion, statelessness and ceaseless persecution, and finally in our times nearly successful genocide, dramatically followed by fulfilment of the never-relinquished dream of return to the homeland. Viewing this strange and singular history, one cannot escape the impression that it must contain some special significance for the history of mankind, that in some way, whether one believes in divine purpose or inscrutable circumstance, the Jews have been singled out to carry the tale of human fate.

Three Christian Views:

King Louis XIV of France asked **Blaise Pascal**, to give him proof of the supernatural. Pascal answered: 'Why, the Jews, your Majesty – the Jews.'[104] Elsewhere[105] he writes:

It is certain that in certain parts of the world we can see a peculiar people, separated from the other peoples of the world, and this is called the Jewish people . . . separated from all the other peoples of the earth, who are the most ancient of all and whose history is earlier by several centuries than the oldest histories we have . . . My encounter with this people amazes me and seems worthy of attention . . . Lovingly and faithfully they hand on this book in which Moses declares that they have been ungrateful towards God throughout their lives, that he knows they will be still more so after his death, but that he calls heaven and earth to witness against them that he told them so often enough.

(NB Pascal's amazement includes the observation that the Jews preserve and transmit a book that is unflattering to them. This surely merits our attention.[106])

---

[103] Barbara Wertheim Tuchman was an American self-trained historian and author. She became best known for *The Guns of August*, a history of the prelude and first month of World War I.

[104] Quoted by Rabbi Blech in http://hnn.us/articles/38887.html. He is Associate Professor of the Talmud at Yeshiva University.

[105] See, for example: http://www.askmusa.org/site/c.ehLKKZPJLuF/b.2794337/ k.6B2B/ Civil_Society_How_Jews_Have_Survived_and_Thrived_Through_the_ Ages.htm.

[106] Pensées 454.

He continues:

> This people are not eminent solely by their antiquity, but are also singular by their duration, which has always continued from their origin till now. For, whereas the nations of Greece and of Italy, of Lacedaemon, of Athens and of Rome, and others who came long after, have long since perished, these ever remain, and in spite of the endeavours of many powerful kings who have a hundred times tried to destroy them, as their historians testify, and as it is easy to conjecture from the natural order of things during so long a space of years, they have nevertheless been preserved (and this preservation has been foretold); and extending from the earliest times to the latest, their history comprehends in its duration all our histories which it preceded by a long time.

Karl Barth, who did not like proofs from nature for the Christian Faith, said of the history of the Jews:

> In fact, if the question of a proof of God is raised, one need merely point to this simple historical fact. For in the person of the Jew there stands a witness before our eyes, the witness of God's covenant with Abraham, Isaac and Jacob and in that way with us all. Even one who does not understand Holy Scripture can see this reminder. And don't you see, the remarkable theological importance, the extraordinary spiritual and sacred significance of the National Socialism (Nazism) that now lies behind us is that right from its roots it was anti-Semitic, that in this movement it was realised with a simple demonic clarity, that the enemy is the Jew. Yes, the enemy in this matter had to be a Jew. In this Jewish nation there really lives to this day the extraordinariness of the revelation of God.[107]

The Anglican Theologian and distinguished Churchman, **Alan Richardson,** in *Christian Apologetics* (1947) SCM, wrote:

> In view of the remarkable history of the Jewish people it ought not to seem strange to us that they should have some unique destiny to fulfil in the providence of God. The history of other nations provides not even a single remote parallel to the phenomenon of Jewish existence down the ages and to this day. What other nation of antiquity has preserved its identity and character as the Jews have done, though exiled from their homeland and dispersed throughout the world? Throughout centuries of persecution the Jewish race has survived the catastrophes which have so often destroyed the national identity of other peoples. Religious or secularised a Jew remains a Jew – a voluntary or

---

[107] *Dogmatics in Outline*, pp. 75-76.

involuntary witness to the truth that is symbolised in the story of God's Covenant with Abraham. This striking fact of the persistence of the Jewish race has long been recognised as important evidence of the truth of the Biblical interpretation of history.[108]

What about the history of the Christian Church?

The New Testament leads us to expect that throughout its history, just like the churches of the New Testament, the Church will have wonderful life mixed with appalling faults.[109] Towards the end of the age many will fall away from the faith and the love of many will grow cold. Nevertheless, by the grace of God, the gospel will spread to all nations.[110] In other words, as this age draws to its close, parts of the world where the Church has been strong will see a major decline in godly faith and parts of the world where the gospel is new will see a major expansion of the faith of Christ.

What about the destiny of the world?

The Bible leads us to expect that wars and natural disasters will be a constant feature of world history. Towards the end of the age we can expect an intensification of these things together with the added dangers of bombardment of the earth by meteors and the like. Jesus tells us that as the time of His Second Coming draws near, wickedness, false prophets, knowledge and travel will greatly increase.[111] (Nothing wrong with the latter two of course.) Evil will not, though, have the final say in the destiny of creation; for beyond the death of Christ was resurrection – a resurrection that enfolds all creation.[112]

What about the world of science?

Although it would be foolish to use science to prove the Bible's world view, it cannot but be heartening to discover that the Bible's teaching about the essential nature of reality, sits more easily with modern science's discoveries about the natural world than would have been possible with the presuppositions of an earlier science. Twentieth-century scientific discoveries about the foundations of the natural world cry out more and more for a Creator and Sustainer. They further reveal a view of created reality in which the heart of the Bible's message can make sense. They are very briefly summarised here:

---

[108] This is an excerpt from a larger passage found from pp. 141-43.
[109] Acts 20:29-30.
[110] Matt 24:9-14.
[111] See Isaiah 24; Joel 2:28ff; Mark 13; Matt 24: 11; Rev 6:13.
[112] Col 1:15-20.

- The universe gives strong indications that it is finite.
- Space-time itself is not just the container of objects and events but part of the fabric of the natural world.
- Physical existence has at its base mathematical information.
- Although the natural world is ordered it is not a deterministic system.
- Even across the bounds of space and time, physical being, at its foundations, is relational – it is more than just a collection of separate particles.
- Life itself is based on information technology way beyond that invented or imagined by human effort.
- The consciousness of animals and the self-consciousness of humans point to a non-materialistic understanding of animal and human experience.

The Bible's world view

1   God is the ground of the rationality of nature. In modern terms we can say that the laws of electricity, magnetism, gravity etc., which are fundamental to the behaviour of all physical things, did not just happen to be what they are, but owe their origin to God. The foundation of these laws is the Logos or Word of God, which expresses the Mind, Will, Grace and Love of God.

2   God is not only the Creator of all things but also their Sustainer. The universe was not merely created and then left to continue in its own way independent of the Creator. At its foundations – as many think is implied by quantum mechanics – the universe is an open system that seems to depend on a greater order beyond itself. Its continuing existence depends upon the grace of God; 'He upholds everything by the word of his power'.[113]

3   Although God is the Creator and Sustainer of all things, he has granted freedom to nature and especially to humans. We really are free. We do not live in a deterministic universe rigidly controlled by physical or Divine laws.

4   God has given to humankind freedom and authority to rule the earth. Our use of them really does influence for good or bad the world of nature with which we relate.

5   There is a continuing interaction between God and nature, God and the history of the world, and God and the story of our individual lives. God speaks, loves, calls to us, and expects a response.

6   The gospel of Christ is that God has made Himself known to humankind in the redemption of the world. This redemption holds together all of space-time so that, even though we are individually responsible for our actions, yet also we are related across the bounds of space and time with God, one another, and the natural world through the archetypal figures of Adam and Christ.

---

[113] Hebrews 1:3.

Chapter 5

Reflections on the presence of evil and suffering on earth and in the 'after life'

First I say something about Judgment at the end of life on earth. If everyone is to go to heaven, then this earthly life would lose its value and it would not matter how cruel to others one had been. It is precisely because life on earth has value that it matters very much how we conduct ourselves and therefore Judgment must be real. That does not necessarily mean that hell exists for the wicked forever. It might mean that. The Bible speaks with more than one voice on this subject. Perhaps this is because God is deliberately ambiguous. He very much wants all to go to heaven so He will not rid us entirely of fear, knowing it might prompt us in the right direction.

Christians may have a response to the problem of suffering in *this* life, but it is something they can never remain untroubled by, and only speak of with trembling lips.

There are two kinds of evil:

1   Moral Evil   Why do people behave badly? Is God to blame for creating us with the capacity for evil? Why does He not stop us doing evil?

2   Natural evil   Why are there natural disasters – such as earthquakes etc. which surely cannot be blamed on us?

Atheists can hardly believe in a real good and evil independent of human opinion, so they generally see each of these as a practical problem to be addressed, rather than as an intellectual problem; for them, disasters happen, and people behave badly, that's all there is to it. It is however an intellectual problem for pantheism (which is the kind of vague popular religion many people would subscribe to if they were pressed). The pantheist does not believe in a Creator God but rather in God as the spiritual dimension of all that there is – a belief which often goes along with some form of re-incarnation.

Here is the problem for the pantheist:

• If the natural world (which contains evil) is part of God, does not that mean that God is partly evil?

• If the natural world is eternal, does not that mean that evil is eternal and there is no salvation?

• Does it make sense to say we should try to escape the cycle of re-incarnation and suffering when we have already had an infinite time?

In response pantheism often denies the reality of evil by saying that the way things are is *'how things are meant to be'* – and then gives us advice on how to cope with suffering in ourselves and others.

Here is the problem for the Christian theist:

- If God is good and powerful why is there evil and suffering?

S/he may respond in the following way:

Moral evil is due to humans misusing their God-given free will. Since God never intended us to be automatons (we would not be human if we were), His will is that we be free, and we have and do misuse our freedom. All of us have been hurt and given hurt. Actually in the context of human sin, I can show forgiveness. Mutual forgiveness raises our humanity. God's full revelation of His own love – the Cross of Christ could only take place in the context of human sin.

But now to **natural evil**. The Christian may respond in the following ways.

1   The capacity for suffering is a necessary by-product of nature.

2   All things, including evil finally contribute to the goodness of the whole. It is precisely the presence of need in humans and other animals that gives me the opportunity for kindness and courage – capacities that are necessary for the development of humanity.

3   God is not indifferent to suffering: *In all our affliction He too is afflicted.*[114] The Cross focuses God's suffering with and for us.

4   The resurrection of Christ is God's final answer to evil, suffering and death. Evil is temporary. Justice, love and truth are eternal.

But what about all the animal suffering that occurred before humans appeared on earth?

This problem has perhaps troubled the most thoughtful Christians. But it assumes that time is uniform. Actually all creation is affected by the misuse of human freedom including the time **before** humans misused their freedom. Time is not absolute and therefore however far we go back in history we will

---

[114]   Isaiah 63:9.

[115]   I gather that the famous theoretical physicist John Wheeler argued for something that was a logical consequence of quantum mechanics – a Participatory Universe. He alleges that human consciousness is needed for the development of the universe even before humans came on the scene! If that is really so then it might explain how a 'fallen' human soul could affect the world of nature before humans existed!

never reach God's time when nature lived in harmony with humans. We live in time which is affected by human sin.[115]

But now a further comment from Lord Hailsham:

What does shock us, is that the innocent suffer so often as the result of the wrongdoing of the guilty. But this is not as paradoxical as it sounds. As the Devil pointed out to the Almighty in the book of Job, if God was always seen to reward the righteous in this world for doing right, it would be seen, and very soon said, that the righteous were only doing right for what they could get out of it. But God does not desire this kind of obedience. He is set on creating beings with a free will, in a world in which they themselves are responsible for the consequences of their own choices, and desires the free obedience of intelligent and reasoning creatures. Only when Job begins to suffer unjustly and still will not curse God is it seen that he does not serve God for what he can get out of it. The suffering of Job, like the Crucifixion and Passion of Christ, is seen to be the consequence, not of Job's own guilt, but of the presence of evil in the world, and the need for it to be seen that good must be pursued for its own sake, even occasionally at personal sacrifice.[116]

God's purpose was to create and redeem human beings so that they would do good for the sake of goodness rather than just for the sake of a reward. So in this world, pain and happiness exist side by side:

1   Pain exists but is defeated in the end.

2   Good people as well as bad suffer but the good are eternally rewarded in another world that they cannot yet see.

3   God shares all our suffering and ultimately triumphs over it.

4   Ultimately goodness, love and mercy reach fulfilment in the context of evil and pain.

Chapter 6
Knowledge of God – Deeply Personal

It is one thing to be convinced that there must be a Great Mind behind the universe and the mystery of human conscious experience, it is another to go beyond that conviction and respond to what we believe. In this chapter we will consider how we come to know God, and how this knowledge (theology) relates to science.

---

[116]   Hailsham, Lord, 1975, *The Door Wherein I Went*, p. 70.

Prayer and the Personal Knowledge of God

Once we are aware that there is probably more to reality than a collection of atoms and physical laws that govern their interactions; and further, once we have recognised that there is probably a Personal Being above all and yet closely related to all things, then the most obvious thing to do is to try to communicate: Lord Hailsham puts it as follows:

> . . . once you have come to the conclusion that there does exist a Person or rather an Entity transcending Person at the heart of the universe, some sort of prayer life is inevitable, and automatic. It is unthinkable that, having reached the point, one should not at least attempt to communicate. When one does seek to communicate one finds at once that one's first thought is not to ask for something . . . There are moments of simple adoration and thankfulness for all the beauty and glory of the world, the goodness of other people. There are moments of horror at the suffering of men, of agony at one's own suffering, of misery and self-accusation at one's past misdeeds or present inadequacy. Ask for things? Why of course. Obviously if one's mind is troubled by this or that, when one collects one's thoughts and submits oneself to the presence of the Divine, the desire of one's heart comes bubbling forth.[117]

Once we have prayed a prayer we are opening our lives to something essentially different from that which can be reached by natural science. And yet this way of knowing is in a sense scientific, if we define scientific method as using ways of knowing that are appropriate to the object that is before us. This is important, for we don't want an impersonal theology where we try to make logical deductions from nature about what God is like, and then make images of Him using our own reasoning skills. That would just be a modern form of idolatry.

The only appropriate way of knowing persons or The Person is by 'methods' appropriate to personal knowledge namely speaking, listening and trusting. That is to say it is by faith. It will lead to a personal knowledge of a Personal Being to whom the whole natural world owes its own being.

As in the knowledge of all persons our knowledge of God will depend on Him revealing His Mind to us. Our fellow humans reveal their mind to us in words as we spend time in their presence. So it is reasonable to speak of God's self-revelation in terms of a Word which we hear when we are in His presence. Our speech to one another reveals our own consciousness and we can speak of our own true self.

---

[117] *The Door Wherein I Went*, pp. 58-59.

As we have seen when we considered the nature of thought and the mind these cannot in principle be reached by studying the physical processes of the brain. 'Qualia' are characteristics of the 'inside-out-world'[118] that cannot be seen from 'outside-looking-in'. The Apostle Paul's words are relevant here and they are worth quoting again:

> For who among men knows the thoughts of a man except the man's spirit within him? In the same way no-one knows the thoughts of God except the Spirit of God. 'For who has known the mind of the Lord that he may instruct him?' But we have the mind of Christ.[119]

To know God we need His own way of revealing Himself to us. So we do not find God by looking at nature, or seek to find Him as part of the data of natural science. Nature prompts us to look away from itself to God who is its Creator.

In all forms of knowing we have to know an object in the way appropriate to its own being. It would be foolish to use a microscope to try to see a star, just as it would be silly to use a telescope to learn about bacteria.

But there is much more to it than that simple example. We must allow the way we think to change if we wish to advance in knowledge.

- If we had continued to believe that the earth is the centre of the universe we would still have found the motions of the celestial bodies a complete mystery.
- If scientists had clung to the seemingly common sense opinion that space and time are infinite containers of objects and events, we would never have grasped the nature of light nor understood how light from distant objects seems to bend round massive objects like our sun.
- If our logic had been governed by the belief that all of matter is made of tiny particles whose behaviour is governed by the fixed laws of physics we would never have understood how electrons seem able to influence one another even over huge distances although there is in principle no way in which they can communicate. We would have been wedded to the opinion that there is no such thing as real freedom and that humanity itself was no more than a complex mechanism.

It is only as scientists are open to question their own fundamental presuppositions that science is able to proceed to a deeper knowledge of reality. In the physical sciences, as they discover a more profound understanding than they had previously imagined, which comes from the very reality they are seeking to know, true understanding of physical reality progresses.

---

[118] As Puddefoot calls them.
[119] 1 Cor 2:11,16.

This is the reason the theologian Karl Barth so strongly rejected natural theology.[120] He believed we could only know God in the way He reveals Himself to us in the Person of Christ as the Scriptures testify about Him. This has led some to criticise Barth for seeming to give the impression that the wonders of nature are completely irrelevant to our knowledge of God.[121]

But do the startling discoveries about the astonishing structure of all creation really have no place in the knowledge of God?

What, according to the Bible, does nature tell us about God?

For since the creation of the world God's invisible qualities – his eternal power and divine nature – have been clearly seen, being understood from what has been made, so that men are without excuse.[122]

That does not mean that we can go on to construct any personal knowledge of God by applying our human logic to His deeds of creation.

Another human example might help. We can talk with friends about another person who is not with us. We may, for example, discuss his achievements. If that person then enters the room where we are, we stop speaking about him. Our choice is now, either to speak to him, listening to what he has to say, or to ignore him. If we choose not to ignore him then true personal knowledge can begin. So it is with our knowledge of God. Only when we are brought to the point where we are willing to listen to Him, theology truly begins.

Although, according to the Bible, nature leaves us without excuse for not seeking God, it is not in the analysis of that nature, using our own reason, that we shall come to know Him. We may, from nature learn something of His deeds, but true knowledge of any person only really starts when we engage in conversation and talk with him.

Science and Theology in Dialogue

This is why science and theology should engage one another in dialogue. Natural theology is not just a prelude to the real thing. The universe is more than the mere stage on which the drama of revelation, redemption and personal faith takes place. The natural world is very much part of the act. John Polkinghorne reminds us that in Newtonian physics space and time were considered the stage

---

[120] See for example pp. 139-40 of Karl Barth, *Church Dogmatics*, II/1, The Doctrine of God, Part 1, trans. T.H.L. Parker et al. (Edinburgh: T. & T. Clark, 1957).

[121] See for example pages 127ff. of Alan Richardson, *Christian Apologetics*, 1947, also Colin Brown, 1967, *Karl Barth and the Christian Message*, pp. 54-62. John Polkinghorne finds Barth's position difficult to accept. (*Reason and Reality*, p. 56)

[122] Romans 1:20.

on which the drama of physical processes took place, so that the geometry of space 'was capable of being pursued in isolation from the mechanics of matter'.[123]

However he continues:

> In General Relativity this is not the case. Space and matter, geometry and physics, impinge upon each other. What we think of as the force of gravity is due to the curvature of space, which is itself due to the distribution of matter. While it may at times be profitable to concentrate one's attention on geometry and at times on matter, one is always conscious that they together form an integrated whole.[124]

He then goes on to agree with T.F. Torrance's contention that 'the same is true for natural and revealed theology'.[125]

He says of Torrance's view:

> His view is congenial to those of us who believe in the unity of knowledge and who consequently think that theology must take account of all that we know about the world in the course of its enquiry.[126]

Why should anyone struggle against openness to God?

Fred Hoyle, who claims not to be a Christian and for many years was a strong supporter of the British Humanist Association, says concerning one of the purposes of his book *The Intelligent Universe* in which he argues for an extra-terrestrial intelligent designer of the universe:

> This indeed is just what orthodox scientists are unwilling to admit. Because there might turn out to be religious connotations, and because orthodox scientists are more concerned with preventing a return to the religious excesses of the past than in looking forward to the truth, the nihilistic outlook . . . has dominated scientific thought throughout the past century. This book is as vigorous a protest against this outlook as I have ever launched.[127]

Whether or not Fred Hoyle is justified in expressing himself so strongly, it is true that the pursuit of ultimate truth does have personal consequences which may tempt the seeker to resist that which he is discovering.

Let us think again of the advance of scientific knowledge. To recap on what we said earlier in this section: the great leaps forward have often come

---

[123] Polkinghorne J., 1988, *Science and Creation*, p. 14.
[124] *Science and Creation*, p. 14.
[125] *Science and Creation*, p. 15.
[126] *Science and Creation*, p. 15
[127] Hoyle Fred, 1983, *The Intelligent Universe*, p. 9.

when men and women have allowed their previously held convictions about the 'logic' of nature to be changed by the sheer pressure of what they are discovering in their observations. This is not always easy for it may mean giving up a whole way of thinking, which up to that point has provided a secure framework for the way they think about the world.

In the knowledge of God we are faced with a similar situation. Any acknowledgement of Him will deeply affect our whole person and call in question the attitudes we have had in each of our lives. This is especially true in our knowledge of God for knowledge of Him is deeply personal. As we have said above, knowledge of God means dialogue.

It will not however be a talk between equals, for He is far greater than we are, and it will be He who sets the agenda, not us. In this relationship we will simply have to trust Him, believing that our Eternal good is near to His heart. That humble and deeply personal trust is what we call faith. It is the appropriate way of knowing. Just as the telescope is appropriate for knowledge of a star, so faith is the appropriate way of knowing God.

It is very difficult, if not impossible, really to know someone from whom we are estranged. Their real needs and the pressures from which they suffer will remain hidden from us. Before true knowledge can grow, there must be reconciliation.[128]

In the Christian revelation that must lead us to the cross.

In our knowledge of God there can be no detached objectivity. 'Man's search for God' can never be a purely academic exercise or an exercise in curiosity. If he wants to keep it on that level he will simply be playing games and avoiding knowledge of reality.

In both science and theology, the subject (the person seeking to know) and the object (the 'thing' we seek to know), are involved in any true advance in knowledge. This has become even more evident in the 20th century since the discovery of relativity and quantum theory. In relativity theory the relationship of velocity between the observer (the subject) and the thing observed (the object) affects the whole time and space reference of the measurements made. In quantum theory the scientist's own consciousness is bound up with the measurements he makes of the quanta.

---

[128] In the latter part of C. S. Lewis's struggle with the reality of God he says: 'For the first time I examined myself with a serious practical purpose. And there I found what appalled me; a zoo of lusts, a bedlam of ambitions, a nursery of fears, a harem of fondled hatreds. My name was legion.' (*Surprised by Joy*, p. 181)

This is relevant to the study of the Bible. If we do not allow our own consciousness or soul to be influenced by the Scripture we are studying, our analysis of Scripture may have the appearance of being scientific, but nevertheless miss the mark completely.

All of us are scientists in the sense that we observe nature. It may only be to wonder at the roses in our garden or to admire the beauty of a sunset followed by a starlit sky. Most, if not all, of us conclude that there must be 'something' behind or beyond it all.

- In all of us there will be times when we do long for it to be true that, at the heart of the universe, is a Personal Being who knows and cares about us.
- Also, though, in all of us there will be times when we wish we could dismiss the thought of God. We would rather be the master of our own souls and ultimately be accountable to no-one. We may also, from time to time hope that death will provide a way into non-existence so that ultimately there will be an escape from the sufferings of the world and our own participation in the guilt of humanity.

It is not just non-religious people who have this negative feeling, nor is it just religious people who have the more positive feeling. At one time or another many, if not all, experience both.

Many ordinary people think that scientists are inherently non-religious. This is a great mistake. After Paul Davies wrote his book *God and the New Physics*, he was surprised to discover that many of his scientific colleagues were Christian believers and regular Church attenders.[129]

Angela Tilby, in her book *Science and the Soul*,[130] tells us that Fred Hoyle, who, as we have noted, is not a Christian believer, says that scientists are obsessed with God and think of Him more than do clergymen![131] This is particularly true among scientists who are asking the ultimate questions such as 'How did the universe begin?' or 'How did life begin?'

Not all scientists ask such questions, though. A professional academic molecular biologist friend whose full time speciality is examining the fundamental structure of life in the amazing DNA molecule, tells me that he once asked his colleagues in the same field how they thought the DNA had ever got started in the beginning. They answered by saying they had never thought of that before![132]

---

[129] Davies P., 1992, *The Mind Of God*, p. 15
[130] Tilby Angela, Science and the Soul (SPCK 1992).
[131] Quoted by Paul Davies in *The Mind of God*, 1992, p. 223.
[132] This only goes to show that however deep we delve into the riches of nature the sheer business of life can keep us from those quiet moments of contemplation when we can really ask the ultimate questions.

Nevertheless, most scientific books that deal with these and similar subjects have plenty of references to God. Occasionally it may be simply to dismiss Him as irrelevant. Even in these anti-theist writings one detects a certain passion about the subject that seems a cover for a deep unease about the professed unbelief.

My evidence for saying this is a short passage in *The Blind Watchmaker*, by Richard Dawkins. He says that until Darwin published his *Origin of Species* in 1859, 'it was not possible to be an intellectually fulfilled atheist'. Although philosophers may have said that no explanation was needed for the complexity of nature, Dawkins believes that in their 'heart of hearts' they knew such an explanation was needed.[133]

Angela Tilby describes her discussions with scientists and others about the program she was making on science and the spiritual. When she approached Jonathan Miller, the 'polymath of theatre, medicine and television' he responded by telling her that he thought religion was a form of mental illness.[134] Richard Dawkins says that religion is akin to a computer virus that has got into the genes of humankind and is now passed on from one generation to another.[135] Dawkins believes natural selection is not aiming at producing anything. It is a blind process that merely preserves random improvements. He therefore has the problem of explaining why humans are religious when he also believes that religion is actually harmful to the individual human being. His invention of the computer virus theory is his way of getting round the problem. One is tempted to wonder whether he is looking for a materialistic explanation for what he is feeling in his own 'heart of hearts'.[136]

Let suppose Dawkins is right that there are physical causes for religious belief. Would that be so surprising since according to him only physical things exist? Therefore all beliefs (including the atheist belief and also the belief that beliefs have physical causes), would have a physical cause. Therefore all beliefs and thinking could be simply explained away.

Tilby tells us later in her book that the scientist Alan Guth told her that scientists liked the now outdated 'Steady State' (the theory that believes that there was no

---

[133] Dawkins R., 1988, *The Blind Watchmaker*, p. 5-6.

[134] Tilby Angela, 1992, *Science and the Soul*, p. 18

[135] His lecture 'Viruses of the Mind' can be read on http://www.andrew-parkin.demon.co.uk/dawkins/viruses.htm

[136] In an interview with the Daily Telegraph (31st August 1993) Dawkins said: 'I have a strongly developed sense of good. But as a biologist I haven't a very well worked out story of where that comes from.'

big-bang and that the universe has always existed), because they assumed it got round the creation problem.[137] All this goes to show that scientists like the rest of us are only human and they do, after all, let their prejudices influence their thinking. Indeed in discussing these matters Paul Davies in *The Mind of God* says:

> Indeed scientists are very emotional people in these matters. There is no greater misconception about scientists than the widespread belief that they are cold, hard soulless individuals.[138]

There are indeed scientists who get very angry at the suggestion that fundamental scientific enquiry must have relevance to belief in that which is beyond the material universe. Angela Tilby even speaks of:

> the fanaticism of some scientists in their shrill reductionism who resist the new world picture with every fibre of their being because it opens them to anxieties they have spent their lives avoiding.[139]

Drusilla Scott comments that to 'shut out of science the very processes by which all knowledge is gained could only be done by men who were afraid.'[140]

Steven Weinberg's *The First Three Minutes* was one of the first books to explore the relationship of the tiny world of particle physics with the opening moments of the genesis of the whole universe. The last pages deal with the end of the universe. It is striking that he cannot not avoid the metaphysical question though he chose (without any attempt to justify his choice) the belief that everything is meaningless. He says:

> The more the universe seems comprehensible the more it seems pointless . . .
> The effort to understand the universe is one of the few things that lifts human life a little above the level of farce, and gives it some of the grace of tragedy.[141]

What really, in the depths of his mind, lies behind this statement? One can only surmise that if he believes that the universe is becoming more and more comprehensible in exclusively materialistic terms, then there is less and less room for the belief that it has purpose from beyond itself. Yet the driving spirit of the scientific enterprise comes from the belief that it is worth knowing about. Without this spirit of science, life would be merely farce – but the efforts of science take it from pure farce to a story which appears to have meaning but can only end in death.

---

[137] Tilby Angela, 1992, *Science and the Soul*, p. 86.
[138] Davies P., 1992, *The Mind Of God*, p. 16.
[139] Tilby Angela, 1992, *Science and the Soul*, p. 100.
[140] Scott Drusilla, 1995, *Everyman Revived – the Common Sense of Michael Polanyi*, p. 41.
[141] Weinburg S., 1977, *The First Three Minutes*, pp. 154-5.

A problem for him is using the word 'tragedy' for 'human life' in that tragedy implies that something with purpose has not realised that purpose. If, in principle, life could have no purpose it would be a farce but could not be tragic!

Einstein spoke about the fact that the universe is comprehensible (that is, that it has a rational structure that can be investigated by minds capable of making the appropriate investigations). As we noted earlier he uses it to criticise atheism:

> And here is the weak point of positivists and professional atheists, who feel happy because they think they have pre-empted not only the world of the divine but also of the miraculous. Curiously we have to be resigned to the miracle [my emphasis] without any legitimate way of getting any further. I have to add the last point explicitly, lest you think that weakened by age I have fallen into the hands of Priests.[142]

So here we have Einstein wanting to combat atheism without falling under the influence of clergymen or other professional religious personages. Elsewhere he says that he does not believe in a *personal* God. Yet he was in the habit of referring to God as the *dear Lord*. This could reflect a struggle in his own mind, although T.F. Torrance argues that his rejection of a personal God was a rejection of anthropomorphic views of a God. That did not mean he believed in an impersonal God but rather in a 'superpersonal' God.[143]

Certainly we see this struggle in the mind of Paul Davies. His first book '*God and the New Physics*' revealed the strange world of sub-atomic physics. In the book he goes backwards and forwards between belief and unbelief.[144] Repeatedly he seems to argue for the existence of God and then to wriggle out of this belief. Significantly he always says he has a feeling of 'unease'[145] about these latter arguments for of course they only push the problem one stage further back.

In the Preface to the book he says that science is a surer route to God than religion.[146] He now says this is not so. In his more recent book '*The Mind of God*' he tells us that science cannot take one to that Reality which is the ultimate explanation of nature.[147] He proposes mysticism as a way to know God.[148]

---

[142] From a letter by Einstein to Maurice Solovine, quoted by John Templeton in *The God Who Would Be Known* (1989) p. 23.

[143] See his unpublished paper, 'Einstein and God'.

[144] This is most evident in Chapter 3.

[145] See for example p. 42.

[146] Davies P., 1984, *God and The New Physics*, p. ix.

[147] See pp. 223-26 of *The Mind Of God*, in which among other things he argues from Godel's theorem.

[148] See pp. 226-29 of *The Mind Of God* in which he obviously prefers to speak of mysticism rather than 'religion' but nevertheless does not rule out Christian theism.

Other well known scientific authors who clearly struggle with the question of God are Stephen Hawking[149] and Fred Hoyle.[150]

Several references have already been made to John Polkinghorne who is not only a scientific author of real distinction but also is a Christian believer who makes very good and successful attempts to bring his faith and science together. In his *Reason and Reality* he speaks of disappointment that there are very few theologians who take an interest in the frontier areas of science.[151]

Just as Paul Davies tells us that false assumptions are often made about the humanity of scientists, there also are popular misconceptions about theologians.

One would expect them all to be on the side of God, the Bible, and the Church. But that is not always the case. There can even be a resistance to any idea that God really does interact with the physical world. So many have devoted their lives to Biblical research with the assumption that there is no real interaction between the physical and the spiritual that a challenge to this produces anger. It is as if they have wanted to maintain academic respectability in our secular age.

Angela Tilby thought some theologians she had met were afraid of dialogue with science. In her undergraduate days at least she judged them to be 'craven and cowardly'.[152] But the individual theologian like the rest of humanity may have conflicting desires within himself – a desire to believe and a desire to be free from belief.

---

[149] There are many instances revealing this in *A Brief History of Time*. For example in his chapter: 'The Origin and fate of the universe' he argues that, with the theories of inflation and 'imaginary time', it is possible to avoid the question of creation (p. 116) and yet in the same chapter, after discussing the Anthropic Principle, he says (p. 127): 'It would be very difficult to explain why the universe should have begun this way, except as the act of a God who intended to create beings like us.' I am not saying he contradicts himself, but rather that he clearly and honestly reveals a mind (and heart?) still wrestling with the subject.

[150] As we have seen in his book *Intelligent Universe* he argues strongly for Intelligent Design and castigates fellow scientists who resist this. Yet even though he strongly argues for extra-terrestrial intelligent design, he certainly does not argue that we should seek personal relationship with this 'creator'. One detects a certain wistfulness though, when, after discussing the horrors of war and the human self-destructive tendencies that according to him come from a materialistic understanding of the universe he says: 'I am not a Christian, nor am I likely to become one as far as I can tell.'

[151] See p. 1 in his Introduction.

[152] Tilby Angela, 1992, *Science and the Soul*, p. 91.

Christians who are academic scientists also may not want to bring the physical and the spiritual together. Paul Davies says they like to keep Sunday for the spiritual and the weekdays for their physical sciences.[153] This may be too hard a judgement because of course it would be silly to expect a Christian chemistry teacher (say) to keep referring to religion in his lectures.

If we really believe that God is the Creator and *Sustainer* of the physical universe, and further that His redemption reconciles our fallen physical world with His Eternal Spirit; in short if we really believe in the incarnation, death and resurrection of the Son of God we must not allow a dualism that breaks up reality into unrelated categories. If we do fall into this dualism, knowledge becomes depersonalised and we cut ourselves off from reality.

Prayer Changes Things?

Chapter 5 of John Polkinghorne's *Quarks Chaos and Christianity* is relevant to this last section. He believes a scientist can pray.

It is only in the relationship of dependence upon God that nature's own order is continually renewed. This does not mean that God keeps wanting to interfere in His creation, adding new laws of nature and suspending others. His respect for all that He has made is too much for that.

John Polkinghorne does not agree with Richard Swinburne that a miracle is a 'non repeatable exception to the operation of nature's laws, brought about by God'.[154] He believes that miracles are 'perceptions of a deeper rationality than that which we encounter in the every day, occasions which make visible a more profound level of Divine activity'.[155]

If he is right, that deeper rationality must surely involve God's redemptive presence and work in His fallen creation – a work which must lie in and behind all His relationship with the world. Miracles must then be a window into that saving presence of God.

When God's people keep demanding more and more miracles He is angry with them for their lack of trust in Him.[156] They want the blessings that a Mighty God can give, without His personal presence. When miracles do occur they must be the exception rather than the rule. They certainly can never be *demanded* by humans as a sign of His presence. The devil would be more willing

---

[153] Davies P. 1992, *The Mind Of God*, p. 15.

[154] Polkinghorne J.,1989, *Science and Providence*, p. 52.

[155] *Science and Providence*, p. 51.

[156] This is a major theme of the Old Testament narratives about the wilderness wanderings of the people of Israel – a theme which is taken up in the New Testament.

to astound people with the 'wonders' he could do. Indeed the great miracle which God does is essentially to reunite a lost world with Himself. It is the miracle of New Creation in the birth, life, death and resurrection of the Son of God. All other miracles of God anticipate it or flow from it.[157]

To explain a little further how a scientist like John Polkinghorne believes 'Prayer Changes Things' I need to say a little about 'Chaos Theory'. Not only in the micro-world of the very tiny is there indeterminacy but also in the macrocosm. It is impossible for weather forecasters ever to give meaningful predictions beyond a few days. This is not because of their inadequate knowledge, but because *infinitely* small variations in initial conditions have large inherently unpredictable consequences.

John Polkinghorne believes that this enables us to understand more clearly how there is room for God, in answer to prayer, not only to sustain the world in being, but also to act within the world – without upsetting the basis of the laws of nature.[158] Effective prayer that 'changes things' he tells us is the alignment of our will with the will of God when we open our wills to His.

This 'laser beam' alignment (as John Polkinghorne goes on to call it) between the purpose of God and the will of humans is a powerful medium through which the purposes of God are accomplished in the world. Because God really has given us freedom in the world to choose between one good and another, our prayer is not just passive acceptance of His will but active participation in it.

He sees God's providential activity not so much as a supernatural 'push' but as information input into nature.[159]

Chapter 7
The Lord's Prayer

At the beginning of this book I quoted the French mathematician and philosopher Blaise Pascal. To remind ourselves, he said:

Men despise religion. They hate it and are afraid it may be true. The cure for this is first to show that religion is not contrary to reason, but worthy of reverence and respect. Next make it attractive, make good men wish it were true, and then show that it is:

---

[157] Matthew 12:38-42.
[158] This is one of the main themes of his Science and Providence.
[159] 1990 J.K.Russell Fellowship Lecture, 'God's Action in the World'.

- Worthy of reverence because it really understands human nature.
- Attractive because it promises true good.

This section is relevant to the last part of his exhortation – 'make it attractive so that good men wish it were true.'

Several years ago I watched a television news/current-affairs program. The presenter was introducing a discussion on the subject of Religious Education in UK schools. He told the sad story of a 13-year-old child who had lost his parents in a road accident. The boy had said to the police that he wanted to pray but did not know any prayers to pray. He had never even been taught the Lord's Prayer!

Our secular age deprives children of many things they need for their developing humanity. That case is just one of many.

Our Father . . .

The God of Christian prayer is not a puppeteer who controls everything. Some religious belief may hold the view that God controls all things. Some seem to believe that 'Not an atom moves unless God pushes it'. If that were our belief, coupled with the added belief that God's ways are unknowable, then no experimental science could ever get off the ground.

On the contrary we do not pray, 'Our dictator which art in heaven', nor 'Our boss who art in heaven', for that would imply that we could earn God's favour as a man/woman earns wages. It is by His grace we live. We can never earn His blessings. Nor do we pray 'Our Prime Minister who art in heaven'. We choose (or should choose) our government leaders but we don't choose which God we are going to address because there is only one. Isaac Newton believed that, since the laws of nature are uniform throughout the universe – the law which governs the fall of an apple is the same law that governs the motions of moons, planets and stars – there must be only one Lawgiver namely the one God.

A good father gives his children as much freedom as he can within certain limits.

There were many trees in the Garden of Eden but only one was forbidden. Some people have very bad fathers. When we say God is Father we don't mean that he is like an earthly father magnified to infinity – for those of us who are fathers are all imperfect.

The Apostle Paul tells us that we bow the knee before the Father from whom every family in heaven and on earth takes its name.[160] That means we don't understand the Fatherhood of God by our experience of earthly fathers

---

[160] Ephesians 3:14.

but that we understand the true meaning the calling of earthly fatherhood by our knowledge of the Eternal Father.

A good father is full of love for his children and is prepared to make sacrifices for them even if their suffering is their own fault. So our heavenly Father made a sacrifice for our sake. Writing of the Cross of Christ, Paul tells us that *'God was in Christ reconciling the world to Himself not counting our trespasses against us.'*[161]

In this we see the greatness of God. He is Almighty, but his greatness and glory is revealed in the Cross. Because God is love, He won't just give us a happy pleasurable time. On the contrary, He has a high destiny for each of us. Quite often that may involve us in painful experiences – just as His care for us means that *'in all our affliction He too is afflicted.'*[162]

We hear that Saddam Hussein was beaten when he was a child by a cruel father. So was Joseph Stalin. That does not excuse what they later did to their own people but it was a factor.

In one of my former congregations we had a Church elder who, in his childhood, had been beaten and beaten by his drunken father. In his late teens he was reaching the end of his tether so he kneeled down by his bed and said the Lord's Prayer. As he was praying he felt the power and love of God, like 'spiritual electricity' flowing through him from feet to head. It changed his life and he became a deeply respected leader of our church. All his sons gave their lives to serving God.

If we believe that there is nothing greater than God, we will seek the same kind of qualities that we believe are in Him. So if people believe that greatness is seen in the ability and desire to control others then they are more likely to seek that for themselves and dictatorships will thrive in such societies.

However if we believe that ultimate reality is a personal Father, then we hold other persons in deep respect and value their freedom as well as our own.

Who art in heaven

In several places in the New Testament we read that Jesus did not merely ascend into the sky but went beyond the skies into heaven itself.[163]

Christ is the meeting place of this world and heaven which is in a greater dimension than we can imagine. If we imagine this world as the X axis and the greater world as the Y axis then where do they meet? At the origin or zero point of the graph.

---

[161] 2 Corinthians 5:19.
[162] Isaiah 63:9.
[163] E.g. Ephesians 4:10; Hebrews 4:14; 7:26.

Another of our Church elders was playing bowls and then he suddenly fell down. His fellow bowlers gathered round and asked him: 'What is the matter Bill?' (I have changed the name for the sake of this piece of writing.) He answered and said: 'Look there is Jesus in heaven'. He had reached the zero point of life on earth and for a moment could see this world (his fellow bowlers and the bowling green) and also he could see into heaven and the link between the two – Jesus. A few days later I conducted Bill's funeral. His fellow bowlers were there and when it was all over they came to see me to tell me what had happened.

But where is heaven? I remember when the first Russian in space returned to earth he remarked that he hadn't seen God! If he had we would have been worried, because that would have meant that God was an object in space alongside other objects like sun, moon and stars.

Here are three petitions concerning God's name, His kingdom, His will:

Hallowed be Thy Name

We are promoted to pray like this:

Lord, Your name is dishonoured in countless television programs, many schools, factories and offices. None of us have the power to restore honour to your name so we ask You to bring honour to Your name.

May this be true in my own life today! Unworthy though I am, may it be true in the life of my family, of my friends, of my neighbourhood, of my Church, nation and – one day – the whole world.

Until that wonderful day comes, may:

Thy Kingdom Come

When James Irwin walked on the moon he reported that he began to pray for the first time in his life. He looked up into the lunar sky and could see the beautiful earth from which he had come. Then he said that on that earth he knew that there were wars and many people starving. There too was his wife with whom he had quarrelled before he began his journey. He must go back to earth and be reconciled to her. Then he said: 'What is more important than man walking on the moon is that God should walk on earth.'

That is the Christian claim. He did and will come. Not just sending messengers or intermediaries. Even prophets can't save us. Only God in our humanity can. That is the belief of Christians about Jesus. Not so much that this man Jesus is God. But that God has entered our humanity and taken the human name Jesus. When among us He healed the sick, forgave the sinner, cast out evil, calmed the forces of nature, brought a severe word of judgement to the self-righteous and proud, and raised the dead. In Him we see a window into the healed creation which will be revealed for the whole earth and all peoples at the end of the age. Then his forgiving, healing, calming, judging and resurrection power will be seen by all. So what was accomplished 2000 years ago in the tiny country of Israel will one day be fulfilled in all the earth.

Too good to be true? Well sometimes it does seem so. However there certainly was a first Creation for here we are and here is a universe in which we live. If it exists then why not hope for a new creation – a renewal of the first?

When that does take place and heaven is re-united with earth then we shall see fulfilled the petition:

Thy Will Be Done on Earth as it is in heaven

There are so many things now that are not the will of God – cancer, all disease, cruelty to humans and animals, partings, sorrow and death. They will be finished forever.

Belief in the will of God implies that there is purpose for human life. This is in contrast to Richard Dawkins' often proclaimed view (for which in principle there could be no evidence) that there is no overarching purpose for our lives. When will this will of God be done? We do not know but there are signs.[164]

1   Over and over again the Old Testament prophets tell us that the history of the Jews will be unlike the history of any other people; towards the end of time, after great suffering, the Jews will return to the Promised Land, where they will become the centre of hostility. This hostility will affect the whole world. Eventually God will reconcile them to their Messiah and cleanse them from their sin.

2   In the Church we can expect a falling away from faith but also a spread of the gospel to the entire world.

3   In the world we can expect many birth pangs as the day of new birth for the world gets nearer and evil gathers in momentum attempting to do its worst – thankfully an attempt which, after a very frightening phase, will fail.

From the New Testament we can learn of at least three ways in which the word 'purpose' is used:

1   But the Pharisees and experts in the law ***rejected God's purpose*** for themselves, because they had not been baptised by John. (Luke 7:30 NIV)

From this we learn that it is possible to reject God's purpose for ourselves.

2   Christ was handed over to you ***by God's set purpose and foreknowledge***, and you, with the help of wicked men, put him to death by nailing him to the cross. (Acts 2:23 NIV)

The death of Christ had been in the purposes of God from the beginning.

---

[164]   I expanded on the three following signs in Chapter 4.

3   And we know that in all things God works for the good of those who love him, who have been called according to his purpose. For those God foreknew he also predestined (purposed) to be **conformed to the likeness of his Son** ... (Rom 8:28-29 NIV)

From this we learn that God's purpose for His people is that we be made like Christ: the Son – not slave – of God.

We should not be anxious about the future but be confident that God's kingdom will come. We should not have worries about the long term. So how should we regard the needs of this *present hour*? We are tempted to worry especially when we see the very obvious dangers the world faces.

Humans have the rational ability (which animals probably don't have) to reflect on our own lives. That can reveal the dark side of our self consciousness. So the remaining petitions relate to our day to day lives in the present.

Give us this day our daily bread

This is a prayer for our daily needs – not luxuries. Now various phrases:

This Day

We are not praying for provisions for the future. We do not know what the future will bring. 'Therefore do not worry about tomorrow, for tomorrow will worry about itself. Each day has enough trouble of its own.' (Matt 6:34)

Of course we must make sensible provision for the future – but should not live in anxiety.

Our prayer for the future is 'Thy Kingdom Come . . .' not 'Lord I am worried about what may become of me in ten year's time.' Rather, 'give me today the strength I need for today'.

Give

Not 'give me' in the sense that 'I don't want to bother to work'. If we are able, we still need to earn our own living. Farmers have to plough and sow and reap to provide basic cereals.

'Give' is an expression of ultimate dependence on God who normally uses human means of provision and distribution. Behind the farmer lies the Creator. All food was once alive and we can't make any living thing.

Daily

This is an expression of day to day dependence.

Just as bread or food is indispensable for the life of body, so *being forgiven and forgiving* is indispensable for the life of soul.

Forgive

Forgive us our trespasses (or debts) as we forgive those who trespass against us (or our debtors).

Before she died in 1988, Marghanita Laski, one of our best known secular humanists and novelists, said in a TV debate with a believer in Christ, 'What I envy most about you Christians is your forgiveness; I have nobody to forgive me.'

Forgive does not mean excuse. 'Excuse me' means please don't hold it against me because it was not my fault. 'Forgive me' means although it definitely was my fault, I am truly sorry, please don't hold it against me.

But how can we possibly confess our own sins properly? We can't. The baptism of Jesus was a baptism of confession of sin. Whose? Those of the whole human race. As our High Priest he takes our prayers and brings them before the Father. Our very inadequate confession is a joining of ourselves to His confession.

True repentance leads to a forgiving spirit. If we are forgiven we will find it easier to forgive others.

That does not mean we should never be angry. Genuine forgiveness does not deny anger but faces it head on. Jesus himself did feel anger at hypocrisy in the religious leadership of Israel – yet on the Cross He prayed for their forgiveness.

'I will not forgive for he had no excuse'. How do we know? We don't know what private pressures and difficulties he may have – also we are not asked to excuse someone but to forgive.

We ask God to forgive the past and put His hand on us for the future. 'Thy Will be done.'

But we ask Him:

Lead us not into temptation

These days the word means 'seduced to sin'. Of course God does not tempt us like that. But in Greek the word means 'test' or 'trial'. God is fashioning us – for He has a high eternal destiny for us.

So how are we to understand the petition: 'Lead us not into temptation'?

Perhaps a clue is found in the Greek word translated 'into' (*eis*) implying in this context 'right inside' so there is nothing to look at but trouble and testing. If this interpretation is correct the phrase means 'don't allow me to be completely engulfed by troubles.'

Yes trials will come. They may in the long term strengthen me. But do not let me be overwhelmed by them. Don't let me be in the situation that wherever

I look there is testing. Even though trials may come, let them not weaken our faith. Let not the devil get hold of our lives. Let us not fall into sin. Instead when dangers come:

Deliver us from evil

Wars, weapons of mass destruction, famines, disease, suffering and death, etc. will not have the final say in the destiny of this marvellous world.

Of course the whole prayer assumes we allow the hand of God upon our lives. 'Thy will be done in us as it is done in heaven' – but we should remember that the hand is the hand of him who is *King of Kings, to whom belongs all power and glory for ever.* Amen.

Appendix 1
Some Difficult Issues in Human Bioethics and a Christian Response

Relevant to this discussion is the nature of the 'soul' or 'self' of the unborn child or the newly fertilised embryo – outside the mother's womb.

I have attempted to show in the preceding chapters that the self or the soul's nature cannot be defined in material terms and therefore provides us with a mystery. However we are undoubtedly speaking of something real which interacts with the physical.

However wise we are in understanding the physical world, we definitely do not have the scientific tools to infer that that there is no definite difference between animal and human. According to surveys, most people are opposed to experiments using human-animal hybrids. They surely recognise that there is a difference between animals and humans – a distinction we must not blur. If we rely entirely on physical characteristics and believe we are simply descended from animals[165] we have no way of making a distinction. We learn from theology that here is a God-determined distinction, and therefore we should do nothing that confuses that distinction, such as experimentation with human-animal hybrids.

Briefly, those who favour giving science freedom to advance in genetic technology emphasise the potential huge medical benefits. Some medical researchers dismiss this as 'hype' saying that all that is claimed for this technology is greatly exaggerated. I am not qualified to engage in this argument. I merely note it.

---

[165] See the appendices on *The Blind Watchmaker* and 'Intelligent Design'.

Those opposed to giving science freedom to advance genetic technology emphasise the sanctity of life at its earliest stage and fear the 'slippery slope' into eugenics.[166]

First I need to say something about Human Reproduction and differentiation. It is important that those who are involved in the ethical discussions should be aware of this scientific point.

In reproduction male sperm and female ovum combine to form a new embryo. The nucleus of this new embryo is a new DNA code, which is derived from both mother and father. For the first 14 days this embryo divides and multiplies but is not a miniature human being. It is more like a 'recipe'.[167] Each cell has the same DNA code. Each cell has the potential to form any part of the body. At 14 days, the cells 'differentiate'. Different parts of the code in each cell are switched off and so each cell now 'knows' what part of the body it is to form. What differentiates a skin cell (say) from a heart cell (say) is the parts of the code that are switched off. At this stage of 'differentiation' (a great mystery)[168] we have the beginnings of a human being in miniature.

We go on to consider a few of the main issues.

---

[166] Eugenics was the attempt by the Nazis to produce the perfect 'race' and therefore they practised a discrimination against the 'imperfect'.

[167] Richard Dawkins' word for this living entity.

[168] Each cell in my body (there are trillions of cells in each human body) contains the same DNA computer program that determines, as I grow in my mother's womb, my physical characteristics. How is it then that, at the time before any of my limbs have begun to form, that cells which become part of my arms (say) know they are there for the benefit of my arms and those in my toes (say) know that they are there for my toes? Biologists call this the problem of 'differentiation' and it is still a great enigma. A very full and technical discussion of research into the riddle of 'embryonic differentiation' is given in an article by Robin Halliday, 1990, (CSIRO Laboratory for Molecular Biology, Sydney, Australia) 'Mechanisms for the Control of Gene Activity During Development'. Is there another plan or control greater than the DNA that is switching on the parts of the DNA relevant to finger growth in the cells of my fingers while keeping the parts of the same DNA that have to do with the growth of other parts of my body switched off? If there is this greater plan where is it located? Please note that although the example of the human nose, fingers and toes are given here, this problem relates to most forms of life.

Many falsely assume that the DNA is merely a scaled down version of the living creature, or that the creature is a scaled up version of the DNA. This is not so.

[continues on the next page]

In Vitro Fertilisation

This is the use of artificial techniques to join an ovum with sperm outside (in vitro) a woman's body to help infertile couples to have children of their own. The basic technique of IVF involves removing ova from a woman's ovaries, fertilising them in the laboratory, and then inserting them into her uterus. The first 'test-tube baby', Mary Louise Brown was born in England in 1978. Many ova are removed from the womb and fertilised. Only one or two are returned to the womb. The remaining ones either are discarded or made available for experiments.

[continued] Research Chemist Ernest Lucas tells us: 'The single fertilised egg does not have miniature arms and legs. These new structures appear later as the cells multiply and divide.' (*Science and the New Age Challenge*, p. 102.) As well as the reason given in the previous paragraph, complicated and wonderful though the DNA may be, it cannot, of itself, account for the enormously greater complexity of many parts of my physical body. Writing about the brain Richard Dawkins, in his preface to *The Blind Watchmaker*, tells us: 'The brain with which you are understanding my words is an array of some ten million kiloneurones (ten thousand million neurones). Many of these billions of nerve cells have each more than a thousand 'electric wires' connecting them to other neurones.' Professor Ambrose in *The Nature and Origin of the Biological World*, p. 152 tells us: '[The brain] is like 500 million telephone exchanges all connected properly. The connections possible are $10^{1,300,000,000,000}$. It might even seem, that in order for the DNA to be changed into an individual life form, a set of mechanisms more complex than the DNA must operate on it. (See Hofstadter D.R., 1980, *Gödel, Escher and Bach*, p. 160.) In this case the various parts of the DNA would serve as triggers for these mechanisms. So where could this greater mechanism be which controls and is controlled by the DNA?!

Paul Davies writes: 'If every molecule of DNA possesses the same global plan for the whole organism, how is it that different cells implement different parts of that plan? Is there, perhaps, a "metaplan" to tell each cell which part of the plan to implement? If so, where is the metaplan located? In the DNA? But this is surely to fall into infinite regress.' (*The Cosmic Blueprint*, p. 103) It was this problem that prompted Rupert Sheldrake — research biochemist and formerly Fellow of Clare College Cambridge — to propose 'morphogenetic fields' that he claimed must surround each living organism influencing their development. He further believed that these fields even transcend the bounds of space and time so that behaviour patterns of previous members of a species affect the development of new members of the species. His theories go so much against the materialist presuppositions of orthodox science that they have been largely rejected. A very good summary and assessment of Sheldrake's views is given by Ernest Lucas, *Science and the New Age Challenge*, 1996, Chapter 8. *[continues on the next page]*

Reproductive Cloning

This is not used for humans yet. A cell is removed from the skin (say) of a mature person and its DNA is put in the nucleus of a new cell (the cell's own nucleus having been removed.) An electric current or chemical is used to fuse the new nucleus with the egg which is 'tricked' into accepting it. This mature differentiated[169] skin DNA then undifferentiates (how this happens is a mystery). Then the new egg is put in the womb.

So now we have an egg with a DNA derived not from a loving relation between male and female but from one person's skin (say). This is one of the main ethical problems of reproductive cloning. The new baby will be a clone or twin of the life that gave cells of skin.

This process was used to produce 'Dolly' the sheep – which died early of old age related illnesses.

Reproductive cloning of humans is dangerous and illegal in the UK and also illegal in most of the world.

Therapeutic Cloning

This is legal in UK but each case needs special permission from the Human Fertilisation and Embryology Authority (HFEA), and formal application to them.

Its procedure is potentially the same procedure as for Reproductive Cloning but the new cell is only allowed to divide and grow up to 14 days – that is still in a pre-differentiated state. In the 14 days cells are 'harvested' and cultured. Being undifferentiated, they can be used indefinitely as (1) a source of tissue for any part of the donor's body or (2) for researching causes of, and cures for, diseases. These undifferentiated cells are called stem cells and have the same DNA code as the donor and therefore there is no danger of rejection of the implanted tissue.

These stem cells are not embryos – detached from the embryo's outer layer, they have no potential to grow into babies. For 14 days the embryo, before being killed, is a source of stem cells.

[continued] However the problem of differentiation remains. It is discussed in illuminating detail throughout Hofstadter's Gödel Escher and Bach, 1980. Paul Davies wonders whether the DNA acts as a 'receiver' rather than the source of the genetic information. (*The Cosmic Blueprint* p. 106.) If he is right where is this greater information? What is its source if not in the individual cell?

[169] For an explanation of 'differentiation' see the extended footnote above.

Ethical issues with therapeutic cloning involve:

(1) The alleged enormous health benefits to be gained.

(2) The status of this undifferentiated embryo – soon to be discarded. Is it human? Is it deserving of some respect but not as a 'human'? Is it deserving of no respect?

Those who deny that it is human say that the pre-differentiated embryo can still be induced to form twins – so it is not one 'self'.

Opponents say there is no need to use artificially produced embryos to get stem cells. They are present in the blood and bone marrow of an adult.

The response is often 'yes' but the embryonic stem cells are more flexible and easier to work with. Potential results from embryonic stem cells are greater than stem cells taken from mature bone marrow.

Embryo and Genetic Screening

Ethical Issues

Should parents know in advance of any potential or certain genetic disease in their unborn baby? For example a childhood disease, or, late onset Huntingdon's or early onset Alzheimer's. Would you like to know about your future? If you were told you had a genetic disease, should you have children? If you already have children should you tell them? Should your insurance company have the right to know? What about information on government databases and identity cards?

Embryo Screening and Abortion

At present abortion for a diagnosed serious disease is allowed up to birth. What counts as serious? Critics fear the slippery slope. Does an easily cured cleft palate count as serious? No, but some abortions have been carried out for that reason.

What about people with genetic defects we know? Should they have been killed in the womb? My wife and I have a niece with a very serious genetic disease. However, although now losing her sight and in a wheel chair she is a happy girl who has brought out a great deal of love in her family.

Saviour Siblings and related ethical issues

Parents have a sick or dying child. A tissue match from a compatible child might cure him/her. Several eggs are taken from the mother's womb (some may have been left over from previous IVF) and a match is sought and found. The match must be compatible and not contain the defective gene of the sick child. The other eggs are discarded.

Will the new child feel it was chosen just for its 'spare parts'? Will it be happy or unhappy that it was born to save another, rather than born only for the normal reasons? Is the new child there as a commodity? Surely its own attitude of self-giving or resentment will determine the answer as to how it develops as a human being.

Designer babies – a Post-Human Future?

If embryos can be selected for qualities that could help a sibling, what about other qualities such as: gender, intelligence, height and athletic ability?

What about future science allowing us to engineer our feelings, eliminating phobias, guilt feelings, feelings of horror at genetic engineering, revulsion that we are no longer human?

The powerful could engineer happy and contented slaves who do not regret the loss of an earlier humanity. Possibilities like these are taken very seriously by some academics especially Dr Nick Bostrom of Oxford University who favours a post-human future as long as the science is guided 'morally'. I asked him: *Who guides the morality?*

A warning is given in Francis Fukuyama's book, *Our Post Human Future*. The book's subject is the biotechnology revolution – its promises and dangers. With developing techniques for genetic engineering and perhaps designer babies, we face the questions: What is it to be human? How do we differentiate between right and wrong?

Fukuyama considers the following approaches to the answers:

a. Religion (we learn from God our true nature)

b. Natural Law (what we discern from nature)

c. Positivism (customs and rules of society – made by us)

He dismisses positivism, skirts round religion and so chooses Natural Law. Fukuyama believes we can discern from nature a 'factor X', the essence of humanity. In his view it consists of a combination of language, emotions, and the ability for abstract reasoning.

He concludes that any biotechnology must not interfere with these characteristics of our species. If they do they will have produced a 'non-human' being. Even if he is right that these qualities *do* constitute true humanity, he does not say why they *should* be valued. Why should humanity be valued?

As philosophers since Hume have realised, one cannot get an 'ought' from an 'is' or 'are'. The statement: 'this is what people ought to be' does not follow from the statement: 'this is what people are'.

A Christian Perspective

Humans should not play God. This is a common objection to biotechnology. However all medical techniques involve interference with the course of a decaying physical nature. Maybe (being in the image of God) we are meant to be creative?

However, when God created creatures in His image for love and fellowship, He did not clone Himself!

Christian theology cannot give all the answers to the difficult ethical questions that face medics and geneticists in their clinics, hospitals, and laboratories. Lord Hailsham reminds us,[170] even if we are under the authority of God, He allows us free will and rational discussion. Perhaps, in many cases, there is no simple right answer.

However we can say certain things about our humanity.

• Genesis 1 teaches us we are made in the Image of God. Our humanity is not an accident.

• The image of God is best seen in Christ who is 'the Image of the Invisible God' (Colossians 1:15).

• Christ's identity with us goes back to his conception in the womb of Mary.

• We are not made as isolated human beings: humanity involves relationship.

• Reproduction should be from a loving committed relationship between a man and woman.

• Our humanity and God's purposes for us go back to before our birth.

• John the Baptist was 'filled with the Spirit, even from his mother's womb.' (Luke 1:15).

A few verses from Psalm 139:

For you formed my inward parts; you knit me together in my mother's womb. I praise you, for I am fearfully and wonderfully made. Wonderful are your works; my soul knows it very well. My frame was not hidden from you, when I was being made in secret, intricately woven in the depths of the earth. Your eyes saw my unformed substance.

It is the exposition of these great facts of theology that should enable doctors and geneticists to have the perspective they need to make the ethical judgements they face.

Christian theology cannot determine all that is right and wrong in biotechnology but it can give the basis needed to have a rational discussion and make difficult decisions.

---

[170] See the quotation on page 48.

Appendix 2

Who is really blind? A consideration of Richard Dawkins' exposition of neo-Darwinism or evolution in his hugely influential *The Blind Watchmaker*

Richard Dawkins is a well known professional Zoologist. He loves public debate and often appears on British television as an exponent of scientific materialistic atheism.

Although this is one of his earlier books it does lay the ground work for theories that provide the background for the atheistic form of neo-Darwinism.[171] It is an exposition of evolution theory. Like many Christians I had no dogmatic objection to evolution. I read this book in order to understand evolution more fully. By the end, I had become an anti-evolutionist. So it was Dawkins who unintentionally converted me to the anti-evolution position that I now find myself espousing.

My own belief is that Darwin's theory was fairly reasonable in his own day. However since the discovery of DNA and RNA it has become impossible.

However Dawkins is often very scathing indeed about those who disagree with him. Some parts of this article are very critical of his arguments but I hope my language is not as strong as his against his opponents.

His very influential book *The Blind Watchmaker* was first published by Longman in 1986. Not long after its publication it was supported and given prominence by a BBC television program. In 1988 it was republished by Penguin. It has also been translated into many languages and has had considerable influence world wide.

He took its title from the Revd William Paley's 19th century writing. William Paley argued that just as a watch does not come into existence by accidental processes but needs a watchmaker, so the complex mechanisms of the natural world could not have come into existence by chance but need a Maker namely God.

The purpose of Dawkins book *The Blind Watchmaker* is to attempt to show that the amazing complexities of life were brought into existence by the process of 'natural selection' which can be understood in purely materialistic terms. There is no need for belief in God.

---

[171] Neo-Darwinism is the theory of evolution that takes into account the discovery of DNA and RNA. Of course Darwin himself did not know of either

Natural selection has no mind or sight of its own. It is therefore 'blind'. Nevertheless he claims to believe it is the controlling process which has produced the incredible complexity of life we see around us today.

Dawkins several times denies that evolution is a random or chance process. However the way he explains his theory does show that chance or random processes do play a very vital role in the whole process.

It was Charles Darwin who was one of the first to recognise this process which is popularly called evolution.

Dawkins argues his case with considerable wit and creative thinking and rightly refutes some of the arguments of opponents of Darwin. Many of his points are penetrating.

His book has received great praise from academics and journalists alike. I fear though, that those who have heaped adulation on the book have been so dazzled by his brilliant style that they have been unable to recognise its serious flaws.

I would not presume to argue with him as a zoologist or biologist. I am not competent to get into all the scientific details. However I can easily follow Dawkins' actual arguments. At their most crucial points they are not scientific and they are not difficult to comprehend. If one can get behind his marvellous and creative rhetoric and listen to the actual case he is making, one will see that it is flawed at its most decisive points.

Dawkins frequently refers to the famous astronomer and writer Fred Hoyle who, as we noted earlier, although not a believer in the God of the Bible, rejects Darwinism and evolution as expounded by biologists such as Dawkins. Hoyle proposes some extra-terrestrial intelligence as the source of life on earth. Dawkins accuses Fred Hoyle of misunderstanding Darwinism. But in fact it is Dawkins who misunderstands Fred Hoyle.

Fred Hoyle is famous for his junkyard illustration. What are the chances of a whirlwind blowing through a junkyard assembling a Jumbo jet from its pieces scattered about the junkyard? Of course there is no chance that it would ever happen.

Fred Hoyle says that life is so so complex that to say it came into existence by chance processes is like saying that the whirlwind assembled the Jumbo jet.

Now Dawkins claims that Fred Hoyle has missed the point. Dawkins says that evolution of such wonderful mechanisms as the 'eye' do not need such a huge 'single step' increase in complexity. Dawkins says that the increase in complexity comes gradually over millions of years. Natural selection is a cumulative process, which weeds out unhelpful changes in a species and preserves those changes most able to help the species to adapt, compete and survive. This indeed is the essence of much of Dawkins' book. Successive increases in complexity are very small but given millions of generations they explain life as it is today.

But has Fred Hoyle really missed the point?

In Fred Hoyle's book *The Intelligent Universe* (published by Michael Joseph in 1983) pp. 18-19, he refers to his junkyard illustration *not* in relation to the formation of an eye but the formation what he believes are the enzymes necessary for life before cumulative selection can start.

Some critics of Hoyle say that he is exaggerating what is needed for the formation of life. Biologists can argue about this and I am not competent to judge between them.

However what is clear is that Hoyle definitely is not talking about the formation of the eye as Dawkins alleges. The junkyard illustration comes at the end of a chapter in which he is discussing the chances of producing the proteins needed by our cells. He tells us that the chances of producing just one protein (which isn't even alive or capable of self-replication) is like a blind-folded man solving a rubic cube by accident. He tells us that such a man would need 100 times the age of the universe to accidentally solve the rubic cube.

Even the simple bacterium is nothing less than a highly complex computer program (the DNA) connected to a highly complex chemical factory (the cytoplasm) with an amazing translation and communication system (the RNA). Even if such a complex mechanism as a bacterium was not needed at first, and even if Hoyle has exagerated the complexity necessary for early proteins, Dawkins admits that the formation of a molecule capable of starting the cumulative selection process needed a huge single-step increase in complexity. This is the subject of his chapter 6 'Origins & Miracles'. He says, 'we cannot escape the need to postulate a *single-step* [his emphasis] chance event in the origin of cumulative selection itself' (p. 140).

Earlier in the book (p. 91) Dawkins says: 'If a complex organ of life is ever found that could not have been formed by numerous successive slight modifications . . . I shall cease to believe in Darwinism.'

(The logic is the same whether we are discussing the origin of an actual 'organ' or whether we are discussing the origin of any highly complex biological entity.)

Two chapters later he acknowledges that the cumulative selection is both very complex and could not have come into existence by cumulative selection. (It is obvious that you can't use 'cumulative selection' to explain the start of 'cumulative selection'!) So if he is consistent to the logic referred to two paragraphs above he should give up Darwinism.

To clarify matters we ask what level of complexity does Dawkins believe is necessary for cumulative selection to get started? Like Fred Hoyle he too has an illustration. It is not the Jumbo jet (in the junkyard) but a Xerox copying machine.

He says that it can copy things but it can't spring into existence all by itself! What is needed in this 'copying machine'? Dawkins tells us it is a 'machine tool' that needs to be guided by RNA. (RNA is a code that is made by the bacterium.) However there is no bacterium at this stage because life has not yet started. Both the RNA and the machine tool have to come into being by the 'single step' that Dawkins says is necessary for this origin of cumulative selection.

Of course the example of the Xerox machine or a watch are only illustrations. Dawkins knows that a Xerox machine cannot come into existence by itself in a 'single step' move. However he likens the problem of the genesis of life to just that.

So what actually is required to arise spontaneously (not gradually)? He tells us that the 'spontaneous arising of DNA or RNA' is what he is trying to explain. (p. 146). He calls this thing that needs to arise in a single step 'life' (p. 139).

So then how does he explain the formation of the cumulative selection, or putting it another way how does he explain how the something comparable to a Xerox machine or a watch came into existence all by themselves?

He uses a simple argument. Although the chances are small, there are so many planets in the universe, perhaps 10^{20} (which means 100 billion billion), that it was likely to happen somewhere and so it did on planet earth!

But is this a valid argument? If Dawkins is right then there is possibly a working machine whose complexity and information content could reasonably be illustrated by the examples of a watch or Xerox machine on another planet somewhere in the universe. Although it is very very unlikely that the forces of nature could have put together these things by accident there are so many billions of planets that it may indeed have happened on one of them. Does the reader believe it possible? No, and you can be sure Dawkins doesn't either.

Some may respond by saying the Xerox machine is just his illustration. Okay, let's put it another way. Suppose now we were to discover writing conveying information, would anyone believe that such a phenomenon would ever come into existence by chance even if there were an infinite number of planets?

Governments are pouring big sums of money into the search for extra-terrestrial intelligent life. What astronomers are looking for is evidence of language coming from distant planets. Regular beeps will be insufficient to prove that intelligent life is the source. Such beeps could be the result of the physical properties of stellar objects.

However if they detect an actual language conveying useful instructions or information about universal mathematical truths such as: 'After 1 and 2 the number 11 is the fourth prime number' (only about 60 letters when put into English) – they will have found intelligence. They will not conclude that it is just a mindless coincidence and that the possible existence of 10^{20} planets explains it without reference to any intelligent source.

Similarly if archaeologists discover meaningful and useful writing on an ancient stone they will not say: 'Oh well there are billions of stones on earth, we don't need to posit intelligence as its source.'

Why do I use this example of useful language? Because, as we noted earlier, Dawkins tells us that RNA or DNA (forms of useful language) had to arise 'spontaneously' (p. 146). Earlier in the book he tells us that 'life' is all about information in words and language. To quote his words again (p. 112):

> What lies at the heart of every living thing is not a fire, warm breath, nor a 'spark of life'. It is information, words, instructions . . . Think of a billion discrete digital characters . . . If you want to understand life, think about information technology.

(Remember that later in his book, on page 139, he starts his explanation of how 'life' got started spontaneously.)

Let's though be generous to Dawkins and assume that he is describing something much more simple than his quote above implies. However, whatever we concede, the analogy of writing does adequately describe his problem.

Speaking of the information content of the simplest cell of life (in the DNA & RNA) the mathematician Douglas R. Hofstadter in a brilliant book said:

> A natural and fundamental question to ask, on learning of these incredibly, intricately interlocking pieces of software and hardware is: 'How did they ever get started in the first place?' . . . from simple molecules to entire cells is almost beyond one's power to imagine. There are various theories on the origin of life. They all run aground on this most central of central questions: 'How did the Genetic Code, along with the mechanisms for its translation, originate?'[172]

We shall come back to the information content of life later on, when we will note that the physical world (not just the living biological world) is also packed with information at its fundamental levels. Judging by his comments on physics in the very first page of his book this most important point seems to have passed Dawkins by.

---

[172] *Godel, Escher, Bach – An Eternal Golden Braid,* Penguin 1979, p. 54.

But let us return to Dawkins' main point in his chapter on Origins. Remember he estimates that there may be 10^20 planets in the universe and that therefore as long as the odds are not more than 10^20 to 1 against the formation of the simplest form of life in a single step move then his theory is OK. He says that these odds are probably 'ample to accommodate the spontaneous arising of DNA or RNA'.

Significantly Dawkins does not even attempt to explain why he thinks 10^20 to 1 is sufficient odds. It is just an assertion he makes. So it is not surprising to read Dawkins' confession on page 158:

> Does it sound to you as though it would need a miracle to make randomly jostling atoms join together into a self replicating molecule? Well, at times it does to me too.

Earlier in the chapter he anticipates this difficulty by saying that to say that God created life would not help because then we are left with the question of the origin of God. Earlier we discussed the fallacy behind this point.

But perhaps Dawkins will say that the first RNA or DNA to appear were simpler than the ones we know of today. Let us consider the E. Coli cell. It could be written thus: CCGTCAGGATT . . . on and on and on for approximately the length of the whole Bible.

This of course cannot be just a jumble of 'letters'. They have to be in precise sequence to instruct the cell to manufacture the particular proteins needed. (To write out the code for a cell in a human being would require about 500 Bibles for each cell).

Now let us for the sake of argument assume that the most primitive RNA or DNA at the beginning of life needed only the length of the New Testament – no, let us be really generous to Dawkins and assume only a few chapters length would be enough. Let us reduce it even further and say we only need a few sentences, totalling 50 letters say, giving useful information.

How long would we expect a monkey to go on typing before he accidentally typed out the right sequence to tell us – not just anything, but something we needed to know? If he typed one letter per second it would still be a time many times greater than the age of the universe.

Dawkins goes to great lengths to describe an experiment on his own computer. What are the chances of random processes in the computer accidentally typing out Dawkins' chosen sentence: '*Me thinks it is a weasel*'. If the computer is given this sentence as a long term goal and if it is allowed to select from each random attempt the most favourable jumble of letters and build upon that, then Dawkins tells us that it would take a mere 40 attempts (or 'generations') to produce something approaching the desired sentence.

(Incidentally 'Me thinks it is a weasel.' is not only very short, it conveys next to no useful information or instruction – unlike even primitive DNA or RNA.)

But, apart from my above comment in parenthesis, we have reached a crucial point. Dawkins acknowledges at this point in his discussion that natural selection does not have any long-term goal. It is 'blind'.

At this point in the book I thought Dawkins was going to show that 'Me thinks it is a weasel' could be reached even without a goal written into the program. But no! He drops the aim of the computer reaching the sentence and changes it for computer drawings (p. 50).

So he turns away from language (however short and simple) and shows how computer drawings can change to resemble insects. But this is to abandon the extremely important point that the supposed development of life is all about the development of language and information.

(Incidentally I do not see why Dawkins is so pleasantly surprised that his computer program produces insect-like pictures. Given his method of selection it is not surprising at all especially as the changes are based on tree-like branching). Even if we grant that a self replicating molecule of this simplicity could exist, so that the process of cumulative selection could begin, then the progress evolution would have to make to reach oak trees, elephants, whales and human beings would be that much greater.

But for the sake of argument, let us grant that a self replicating RNA or DNA molecule did come into existence by chance processes in the single step move that Dawkins acknowledges was necessary. It is from this basic constituent of 'life' (as we have seen this is the word Dawkins uses on page 139) that the necessary process of evolution is supposed to have started. How does this basic form of life (with no leaves, roots, bones, eyes, ears, feathers, fur, teeth, claws, lungs, heart, brain etc. etc.) change into the amazing variety of plant, animal and human life all around us today.

Dawkins believes that chance processes bring mutations (changes) that cause the variety of life to evolve from the first cell of life. The chance processes are random changes in the DNA code which can occur when a 'parent' brings forth offspring.

Occasionally copying errors occur and so a random change occurs in the following generation's DNA code. These infrequent changes usually produce harmful or lethal effects in the species but occasionally produce beneficial changes for the next generation. (It is extremely unlikely that a copying error randomly made by a typist will improve a manuscript – but Dawkins assures us that this does happen from time to time with the DNA and so we must believe him).

Beneficial changes are obviously more fit to survive and so they do and pass on their new benefits to succeeding generations . . . and so the process of evolution of species continues on. He rightly rules out the possibility of large-scale changes taking place in one single step move.

It is on this point that he so strongly disagrees with his fellow world famous evolutionary biologist: Stephen Jay Gould. Gould like Dawkins does not want God in the picture. However Gould points out that the fossil record shows relatively sudden appearances of well developed life. Gould believes that this shows that large scale changes did take place very quickly indeed – relatively speaking.

Dawkins accepts that the fossil record does seem to show this. However he can't accept it. He says that it is giving ground to the creationists (p. 230). (By the way is the argument that Gould is helping the creationists a scientific argument or an argument of guilt by association?!) This 'Dawkins-Gould' argument is not part of my main thesis so I only mention it in passing. The reader can find Dawkins' criticism of Gould in his Chapter 9.

Fundamental to his book is that small changes that accumulate over many generations can explain the incredible complexity we see in life today. How many generations? He reckons that the age of the planet earth will allow us 100 million (10^8) generations. Is this enough? Let us consider one example – the human brain.

Prof. Ambrose (Emeritus Professor of Biology in London University) in his book *The Nature and Origin of the Biological World*, published by Ellis Horwood 1982, p. 152, describes the complexity of the brain as like 500 million telephone exchanges all connected properly. The connections possible are $10^{1,300,000,000,000}$. (To write this number out in the normal form l, 000, 000 . . . etc. would take about one hundred thousand years to do.)

You might imagine Dawkins would not agree with Professor Ambrose's description of the brain? But he does agree! He writes on the first page of the preface:

The brain with which you are understanding my words is an array of some ten million kiloneurones. Many of these billions of nerve cells have each more than a thousand 'electric wires' connecting them to other neurones.

Now to suggest as Dawkins does that only 100 million generations of small changes could produce such complexity is absurd. And of course the brain is only one amongst countless wonders of the living world. Dawkins himself gives us a description of the wonders of the eye (pp. 16-17), and the sonar skills of the bat (Chapter 2).

Does he really believe 10^8 generations are enough to explain all this?

Elsewhere in his book he tells us that the DNA that controls the Willow tree has as much information as thirty volumes of the Encyclopaedia Britannica. His sentence 'Me thinks it is a weasel' is a very very feeble and inadequate starting point for life even given 100 million generations, especially, as he acknowledges, natural selection is not aiming at producing anything. It is a blind process that merely preserves random improvements. Can such wonderful order really have arisen without an Intelligent Mind bringing it to being?

Now I want to go on to comment about the origin of the order we see everywhere around us. The science of 'order' is not simple. There are many different kinds of 'order'. For example the complexity of a Jumbo jet is very different from the order of such letters we might find such as ABC ABC ABC — on and on and on. If we found such 'writing' (regular but conveying no useful instruction or information) we would still assume that it had not come into existence by chance. It must have been produced by a simple mathematical instruction or physical process — but not necessarily by an intelligent mind. Nevertheless we would still be forced to ask the question as to why physical things have certain properties (and not others) which produce this order, or alternatively, who wrote the mathematical algorithm?

It is only a superficial conclusion that 'mind' is not needed. When we press the question, asking 'Why this and not that?' we can't avoid *mind* as the ultimate origin of all things. More of this below.

However, as noted earlier, if we discovered writing not having a regular pattern (like ABC ABC ABC etc. etc.), but instead conveying useful instructions, (like a language or code) that would be different. We would immediately assume intelligent mind was its ultimate origin.

These issues relating to very different kinds or complexity and order are explored very fully in Paul Davies: *The Fifth Miracle*. He relates his study to the issues of life and biology — issues that we have been discussing in this review of The Blind Watchmaker. Although Paul Davies claims no particular religious commitment I certainly recommend his book for careful study.

The underlying assumption of all modern science (an assumption I accept) is that physical existence has a rational structure open to investigation by science. Certain effects have certain causes because of the way nature is. Experiment is necessary to find these causes because nature did not have to be as it is by logical necessity but its 'order' was chosen for it by its Creator. If we want to discover the order of nature we must go and take a look, i.e. do experiments. A good case, worth considering, has been made by several scientists (e.g. Professor Peter Hodgson — Nuclear Physics, Oxford University) that cultures which did not have a belief in free creation by a single Creator were not able to let experimental science get off the ground.

I wonder if this is what Einstein meant when he said: *Science without religion is lame?*

However as the arch sceptical philosopher David Hume showed we cannot assume that effects have causes unless we believe in 'laws of nature'. He argued that we cannot, by observation, conclude that there are such laws and therefore we cannot assume that, because event A has previously always followed event B, it will continue to do so tomorrow.

Although Hume's argument is difficult to counter, almost all of us do assume that such 'laws' exist. Many (such as Isaac Newton) argued that such an assumption is based on the religious belief that there is one Law Giver.

The 'laws of nature' or rather the rational structure of nature depends on Something beyond mere physical existence. This is what the ancient Greek philosophers realised when they noted that nature has structure and concluded that it must be infused with a non physical element: 'mind' or 'nous'.

Einstein again: 'The only incomprehensible thing about the universe is that it is comprehensible.' It was this obvious rational comprehensible structure that gave him (in his later life) a case against those who thought physical existence alone could explain everything.

A more modern author, who with Dawkins, is a founder of 'sociobiology' is Edward Wilson. He, like Dawkins, believes that the whole of reality can be explained by reductionist science. In a short passage in his prize winning book Consilience he wonders why the universe is ordered. He writes of the 'fortunate comprehensibility of the universe', and says of the world that it is 'surprisingly well ordered' (p. 50). He gives no explanation for this 'fortunate comprehensibility of the universe'. Indeed he cannot.

If we close our hearts and minds to the Eternal Word then we close our minds to Ultimate Reality and the Source of nature's wonderful order. We may look for other ways of knowing ultimate reality but we will be ever closed to its truth. But why should we want that?

Appendix 3
The Intelligent Design Movement

The present day argument, considered here, is between those who hold to so-called Intelligent Design and those who accept the prevailing opinion that natural processes alone can account for two things (a) biogenesis – the origin of life (before the alleged processes of evolution could get started) and (b) the subsequent development of life.

At the outset I should say that personally I prefer the term 'Mind' to 'Intelligent Design' because there is a history of thought going back thousands of years linking non-material mind with matter in various relationships. For example in our own time Roger Penrose FRS, formerly professor of Maths at Oxford, believes that a non-material transcendent reality is the source of all truth, beauty and goodness.[173] The term intelligent designer is probably included in this view of the transcendent world but the source of matter and life is much greter than this. However, for the purposes of this paper, I will be referring to the modern term 'Intelligent Design' (ID).

Opponents of ID include many Jews and Christians – even evangelical Christians[174] – who believe that natural processes for the origin of life and evolution can be reconciled with Genesis 1. They usually hold that the matter of the universe including the natural laws of nature (such as gravity) were created by God and finally tuned to allow, stars, galaxies, planets like earth, and then life to form. In this view God endowed His creation with a 'fruitful potentiality' to produce all that we see around us today. (For short we refer to this view as TE meaning Theistic Evolution or Theistic Evolutionist.)

The first group says that life is so complex and information-rich, that an Intelligent Design is needed to explain it.

An important part of the argument is that the complexity of the simplest form of life contains information in the form of 'code' or 'words' or 'language' (DNA and RNA for example). It is contended that the origin of

---

[173] *Road to Reality*, Chapter 1.

[174] Written from a Christian standpoint, an impressive book criticising ID is *Rebuilding the Matrix*, by Denis Alexander, published 2005.

any code has to be Mind. If one is examining ancient markings on a rock, which are not just complex patterns but a language, one will conclude that they are the products of an intelligent mind. A detailed support for this view comes from the mathematician Bill Dembski who has written extensively on mathematics and information.

Advocates of ID are not proposing a belief in a young earth or a particular religion,[175] even though some of them may hold also to a young earth view that the earth is less than 10,000 years old. They simply are saying that life requires Mind for its origin and also its development as the amount of its information content increases. (There is more information in the DNA of an elephant than of a bacterium.)

Against this view is the view of evolutionists and theistic evolutionists that the ID people are invoking the 'god of the gaps'. It is true, they say, that there is no viable theory of the origin of life – but one should not put any 'god' in that gap to explain it. Science is about finding physical causes for physical phenomena, not invoking God every time science is faced with a mystery.

Those holding to TE say that to invoke God to explain part of creation is to attempt to introduce Him as part of the data of natural science and that is unacceptable. The Jewish/Christian doctrine of Creation says creation is separate from God and therefore one must not look for God in Creation.

To summarise so far: whereas naturalistic science says science is defined as that study which always looks for physical explanations, ID says 'no', science means 'follow the evidence' and the evidence leads to ID.

It might be wiser for ID to argue like this: as Einstein recognised, science examines the rational structure of the material world but it can't explain why it is rational – or has the fundamental properties that it does.[176] (He said: The only thing incomprehensible about the universe is that it is comprehensible.) The intelligent (Einstein's word) non-material source of matter's rational structure, he called 'The Old One' or 'The Dear Lord'.

---

[175] E.g. professors Antony Flew and Steve Fuller support ID and yet have no religious commitment.

[176] Richard Dawkins asks, 'Why are the laws of physics the way they are? Why are there laws at all? Why is there a universe at all? Once again, the lure of "design" is tempting'. (Article in the Guardian, 8th February 2008)

It seems to me that ID is just taking this one step further. It is saying that the properties of the *living* world cannot be reduced to the properties (rational structure) of the *non-living* material world,[177] but has a rational structure of its own. The Laws of Biology, though transcending the laws of physics/chemistry, obey those laws where they operate. In the same way an engineer who builds a bridge must obey the laws of physics, but one cannot go from physics to the bridge – the designs of the engineer have their part as well as the physics governing the properties of the metals etc.

ID maintains that the origin and nature and development of life (the subject of biology) needs non-material and intelligent Mind as its source.

It holds that in the final analysis materialist explanations for any physical phenomenon are inadequate. The answers to the questions '*What is matter?*' and '*What is energy?*' raise fundamental mysteries about the nature and the origin of the intelligibility of all material existence. Biological complexity is just one particularly striking example of this.

Science

ID proponents hold that all of nature points to Mind. However its main interest is in two things namely:

- The origin of life or self-replicating molecules.
- The development of life.

1   Science reveals the inner workings of the simplest forms of life *to be composed of intricate circuits, miniaturised motors and enough digital code to fill an encyclopaedia.* All these things exist in a cell without any brain, nervous system, liver, eyes, ears, blood, lungs, leaves, feathers, bark, roots, petals, etc. Digital code is a form of language and all languages arise from mind. Writing cannot be accounted for from the chemistry of the ink and paper (say) but must have its origin in mind.

2   All the above must have been present before the alleged processes of evolution could get started.

3   ID people also doubt evolution as an explanation for the whole history of life. Random mutation through the sieve of natural selection may be able to account for small changes in living organisms. However sustainable mutations have their limits.

---

[177] This seems to be what the famous theoretical physicist Erwin Schrödinger was saying in the first few pages of his *What is Life?*

4   At present these changes cannot account for the huge changes from a simple bacterium to all the life forms (including ourselves) that we see around us. This ought to be acknowledged publicly. Maybe this alleged process will be better understood in the future. However this hope is based on an unprovable metaphysic.[178]

5   Gödel said that mechanism in biology is a prejudice of his time which will be disproved. In this case one disproval, in Gödel's opinion, will consist in a mathematical theorem to the effect that the formation within geological times of a human body by the laws of physics (or any other laws of a similar nature), starting from a random distribution of elementary particles and the field, is about as unlikely as the separation by chance of the atmosphere into its components.

6   ID proponents say there are mathematical tests for design in the origin and development of life. They show that the type of complexity found in biological systems cannot be the result of mindless algorithms or the properties of matter but must have intelligent mind as its source. For example language needs a mind and we find codes (types of language) in all living things.

7   The world famous atheist philosopher, Professor Anthony Flew, has given up atheism for theism. What is the basis for his change of mind? The extraordinary complexity of the supposed 'simple' form of life discovered by modern biology. In a Philosophy Journal which interviewed him he says:

> It seems to me that Richard Dawkins constantly overlooks the fact that Darwin himself, in the fourteenth chapter of The Origin of Species,

---

[178] One of the most important evolutionary explanations for life's start posits that RNA molecules, which possessed both information storage capacity and catalytic properties, preceded the DNA-and-protein world of contemporary biochemistry. This so-called 'RNA World' hypothesis rescues the evolutionary paradigm from the chicken-and-egg paradox that naturally arises because of the interdependence of DNA and proteins. For the RNA World model to have merit, origin-of-life researchers need to demonstrate that RNA's components can be produced under conditions applicable to early Earth. For RNA molecules to be produced, a chemical pathway to attach phosphate groups to the sugar ribose must operate under the conditions of the primordial Earth. New research demonstrates that no such pathway appears to exist. As origin-of-life researcher Leslie Orgel has stated, 'It would be a miracle if a strand of RNA ever appeared on the early Earth.'

pointed out that his whole argument began with a being which already possessed reproductive powers. This is the creature the evolution of which a truly comprehensive theory of evolution must give some account. Darwin himself was well aware that he had not produced such an account. It now seems to me that the findings of more than fifty years of DNA research have provided materials for a new and enormously powerful argument [for] design.

8   Fosssil Record. A quote from Stephen J. Gould:

Gradualism was never 'proved from the rocks' by Lyell and Darwin, but was rather imposed as a bias upon nature . . . has had a profoundly negative impact by stifling hypotheses and by closing the minds of a profession toward reasonable empirical alternatives to the dogma of gradualism . . . Lyell won with rhetoric what he could not carry with data.'[179]

Philosophy

What exists? (Ontology)

Resistance to the ID view comes from (a) those who deny that non-physical entities exist or (b) those who hold that non-physical entities may exist but do not affect the physical.

Since physical science examines physical things there could be no evidence to support position (a). Position (b) only could have support if it could be shown that the physical universe is a closed system of cause and effect – nothing non-physical affecting what goes on in it. If physics provided us with a TOE (Theory of Everything) it would have gone along way to reaching that goal. However there are several problems, for example:

(a) The advance of science reveals more and more mystery.

(b) Many have argued from Godel's theorem that it can be proved that the universe will never be understood from within itself alone.

Origins

It makes no sense to say that the origin of matter and energy is matter or energy. Since personal beings (with minds) certainly exist in the universe, it is reasonable to believe that the origin of all reality, at least, must be Personal Mind.

---

[179] Stephen J. Gould, 'Toward the vindication of punctuational change' in W.A. Berggren and J.A. van Couvering (eds.): *Catastrophes and Earth History: The New Uniformitarianism*, Princeton University Press, Princeton (New Jersey), pp. 14-16, 1984.

Mind and Matter

ID holds the view that non-material minds have effects in the physical world. Therefore we should be unsurprised that the Eternal Mind also affects the physical world.

Thinking (what minds do) cannot be simply the sum of material processes. If we discover a physical cause (say a virus in the brain) for a belief or a thought then that belief and thought would lose its value.

If all our thoughts were *exclusively* the movement of physical entities in our brains, then there would be no way, by thinking, of determining which 'thought' was correct and which was incorrect since that determining by thinking, itself would be a mere physical process.

One difference between physical events and thoughts of the mind: any physical process, unlike a thought, is neither true nor false, it just is. However thoughts may have the additional property of being true or false. So thoughts cannot be identical to physical processes or a combination of exclusively physical processes.

For example a river running through a valley is neither true nor false (though thoughts about the flow of the river may be true or false). Its running through the valley just exists. Thus there is a fundamental distinction between physical processes (such as the flow of water), which merely exist, and thoughts, which not only exist but also may be true or false. Thus thoughts cannot be mere physical processes.

Bertrand Russell said:

> If we imagine a world of mere matter, there would be no room for falsehood in such a world, and although it would contain what may be called 'facts', it would not contain any truths, in the sense in which truths are things of the same kind as falsehoods. In fact, truth and falsehood are properties of beliefs and statements: hence a world of mere matter, since it would contain no beliefs or statements, would also contain no truth or falsehood. [180]

As we have seen earlier *messages, languages, and coded information ONLY come from minds.* (Minds are conscious – minds that have agreed on an alphabet and a meaning of words and sentences which express both desire and intent.)

The atheist Richard Dawkins writes:

> What lies at the heart of every living thing is not a fire, warm breath, nor a 'spark of life'. It is information, words, instructions . . . Think of a billion discrete digital characters . . . If you want to understand life, think about information technology.[181]

---

[180] Bertrand Russell, *The Problems of Philosophy*, p. 70.
[181] *The Blind Watchmaker*, p. 112.

If we analyze language with advanced mathematics and engineering communication theory, we can say:

> Messages, languages and coded information never come from anything else besides a mind. No-one has ever produced a single example of a message that did not come from a mind.

Languages etc. can be *carried* by matter or energy (eg sounds, ink, electronic and radio signals) but they are none of these things. Indeed they are not matter or energy at all. They are not 'physical'.

The physical universe can create fascinating patterns – snowflakes, crystals, stalactites, tornados, turbulence and cloud formations etc. But non-living and non-conscious things cannot create language. They cannot create codes.[182]

Drusilla Scott tells us of Michael Polanyi's reaction to the claim that the discovery of the DNA double helix is the final proof that living things are physically and chemically determined. No, said Polanyi, it proves the opposite. No arrangement of physical units can be a code and convey information unless the order of its units is not fixed by its physical chemical make-up. His example is a railway station on the Welsh border where an arrangement of pebbles on a bank spelled the message – 'Welcome to Wales by British Rail':

> This information content of pebbles clearly showed that their arrangement was not due to their physical chemical interaction but to a purpose on the part of the stationmaster . . . The arrangement of the DNA could have come about chance, just as the pebbles on that station could have rolled down a hillside and arranged themselves in the worlds of the message, but it would be bizarre to maintain that this was so . . . [183]

Of course many committed to materialism (without evidence) insist that the mind is no more than an aspect of the physical brain/nervous system. We should remember the words of Gödel: 'That the mind is the brain is the great prejudice of our age.'

Mind and Matter interact

My thoughts (non-physical) may affect the physical river if I decide to have go for a swim in it. I make a splash. So our everyday experience of thinking (and deciding) can affect the physical world – making us move our physical bodies and other things too. Thus minds can and do affect physical reality. This was Karl Popper's argument. How mind acts on matter remains a mystery.

---

[182] I owe the wording of the previous two paragraphs to an article that was sponsored by 'Reasons to Believe.'

[183] Scott Drusilla, 1995, *Everyman Revived – the Common Sense of Michael Polanyi*, pp. 116-17.

ID believes not only that the origin of matter comes from non-material mind, but that that Mind continues to act in its/His creation.

John Polkinghorne believes that God's action in the material world does not involve an extra 'push' but an input of information.

This means that the physical sciences are bound to reach points in their research when they come up against a brick wall. They are right to search for physical explanations, but they must have in the back of their minds the fact that all materialist explanations are ultimately inadequate to account for the existence and properties of the physical world.

Theological and Biblical Argument

The Bible teaches that it is not uncreated impersonal particles/energies/laws of physics that are the eternal origin of all things, but an Uncreated Mind or Word who seeks to know and be known. This is how the New Testament puts it:

> In the beginning was the Word, and the Word was with God, and the Word was God. He was in the beginning with God. All things were made through him, and without him was not any thing made that was made. And the Word became flesh and dwelt among us, and we have seen his glory, glory as of the only Son from the Father, full of grace and truth.[184]

ID people may have different interpretations of Genesis 1, but they believe that the Creation was not one event. There were a small number of stages. Among these were (1) Matter-Energy, (2) Non-conscious life, (3) Conscious life and (4) Conscious life that is capable of abstract reasoning.

This means that the sciences should expect to find discontinuities in their examination of nature.

1   The understanding of matter and energy cannot be reduced to 'nothing'.

2   The understanding of non-conscious life cannot be reduced to a complex form of matter and energy. (Biology cannot be wholly reduced to chemistry and physics).

3   The understanding of conscious life cannot be wholly reduced to a complex form of non-conscious life.

4   The understanding of abstract reasoning cannot be reduced to the consciousness of animals.

These are the discontinuities that those who take Genesis 1 to apply to the physical world should expect to find. We should not expect to find that nature is 'one seamless whole' – see below.

---

[184] John 1:3,14.

POSTSCRIPT – FURTHER CONSIDERATIONS

Second Law of Thermodynamics

Opponents of evolution often quote this law which predicts the deterioration of order. Evolution seems to go against this because it posits an increase in order. Evolutionists often make the point that the Law only applies to closed systems. In some circumstances order can actually increase if the system is open to a greater order from which its draws order. So it in contended that the earth is open to the wider universe. But this argument assumes that the universe is itself orderly. So that leaves us with the question as to where its order came from originally.

Junk DNA and Vestigial Organs.

It is commonly claimed that present day creatures have useless parts of their DNA or anatomy which are left-overs from their distant ancestors. However as time goes on, what was once thought to be useless, is, after all, discovered to have function (e.g. tonsils and the appendix). Also it is not completely clear that our all our supposed ancestors did have these extra parts. Since our science is in its infancy in this area, we should hesitate before using this as evidence for or against evolution.[185]

---

[185] One important example where acceptance of evolution has hindered medical practice is advice given to sufferers of back problems. During the 1960s and 70s some medical scientists developed the idea that back problems could be treated through adoption of an unnatural posture. This was a result of the evolutionary assumption that the human spine was an imperfect design, still in the process of evolving from four-footed animals to bipedal human beings. Dr Paul Williams* developed flexion exercises on this basis to reverse or reduce the lordosis curve in the lower back. This proved to be the wrong treatment with sufferers continuing in pain.

Later research by Robin McKenzie** showed that the shape of the spine is a natural design for upright posture, and maintaining the lordosis curve improved the health of sufferers. Treatments have more recently been developed that support the perfectly designed lordosis curve, and recognition of perfect human design has proven medical benefits.***

* Williams, P.C., *The Lumbosacral Spine; Emphasizing Conservative Management*, McGraw-Hill Book Company, New York, 1965.

** See for instance: McKenzie, R., *Mechanical Diagnosis and Therapy for Low Back Pain: Toward a Better Understanding*, Spinal Publications, Waikanae, New Zealand, Saunders, Philadelphia, 2nd Edition, 1996.

*** See for instance: Bergman, J., 'Back problems: how Darwinism misled researchers', AiG TJ, 15(3) pp. 79-84, December 2001.

The Argument from Design – Bertrand Russell and David Hume

Russell

Bertrand Russell greatly respected the argument from design especially as expounded by Leibniz. (He regarded Leibniz, in whom he specialised, as 'one of the supreme intellects of all time'.) Russell writes:

> This argument contends that, on a survey of the known world, we find things which cannot plausibly be explained as the product of blind natural forces, but are much more reasonably to be regarded as evidences of a beneficent purpose.

He regards this familiar argument as having 'no formal logical defect'. He rightly points out that it does not prove the infinite or good God of normal religious belief but nevertheless says, that if true (and Russell does not give any argument against it), it demonstrates that God is 'vastly wiser and more powerful than we are'.[186]

Hume[187]

It is important to appreciate that, religious sceptic though he was (but not one who ever characterised himself as an atheist), Hume shows no sympathy to the approach we are calling 'methodological materialism'. That is, in Hume there is no trace of the idea that teleological concepts such as 'intelligence' and 'design' are inappropriate on methodological grounds in the context of biological explanation. As was usually the case with thinkers prior to Darwin, the basic question for Hume was how much soundly based knowledge can the Argument from Design yield. In Hume's view, in turns out, the answer to this most general of questions is 'not as much as previous philosophers have hitherto imagined', but this conclusion does not depend in any way on the notion that the concept of 'design' itself is in some sense inadmissible at the outset of an investigation into the features and origin of organic nature.

What is Hume's most general verdict on natural theological reasoning? The third sentence of his earlier work *The Natural History of Religion* of 1751 will surprise those who, without properly studying him, hail Hume as a committed metaphysical atheist. Hume in fact writes as follows:

> The whole frame of nature bespeaks an intelligent author; and no rational enquirer can, after serious reflection, suspend his belief a moment with regard to the primary principles of genuine Theism and Religion.

---

[186] See his chapter on Leibniz in his *History of Western Philosophy*.

[187] I owe this section on Hume to Dr T. S. Torrance, retired senior lecturer in Economics and Philosophy at Heriot-Watt University.

How do you detect Design? – there is no scientific test

How do you prove the Forth Road Bridge and similar structures were designed? Is there a scientific test? Does the theory make any predictions? Indeed there are written records of how they were designed. But, says the sceptic:

Perhaps the records were just made up! Maybe the naturally occurring metals just rolled down the hilly countryside and just came together to form a bridge. It's true that we don't understand it all – but we will do one day, without having to invoke the superstitious view that it had something to do with civil engineers. I am not going to believe in the existence of civil engineers until you show me something that they actually do.

ID – a threat to science?

Some allege that it is. But what do they mean? They are usually unconsciously using a definition of science which says it is that subject which only looks for physical causes for physical effects.

But what is the basis of that definition? It assumes that physical nature is a closed system of cause and effect. However we can't assume that. There is no evidence for that belief. As we have seen some have argued from an interpretation of Godel's theorem that the physical world is not a closed system. Why not define science as that discipline which seeks to explain physical effects by following the evidence wherever it leads rather than be bound by an unprovable metaphysics which denies that non-physical realities impinge upon the physical world?

One seamless whole?

It is often claimed by theistic evolutionists and atheists (e.g. Denis Alexander and Richard Dawkins) that nature is 'one seamless whole'. That is to say it must be regarded as one without the need to postulate further creative acts. But what is the basis of this belief? It isn't scientific because science has not shown it to be true – there is still no viable theory of how lifeless matter turned into living organisms. It is not philosophical because there is no convincing ontology to give a basis for the belief.[188] It is not theological because the Bible does not teach it. It is a prejudice.

---

[188] Contrary to this conviction, Bertrand Russell wrote: 'Academic philosophers, ever since the time of Parmenides, have believed the world is a unity. The most fundamental of my intellectual beliefs is that this is rubbish. I think the universe is all spots and jumps, without continuity, without coherence or orderliness or any of the other properties that governesses love.' (Quoted in the Introduction and Summary of *My Philosophical Development* by Bertrand Russell, p. 199)

God of the gaps

It is often alleged that ID people are evoking the dreaded 'god of the gaps'. This criticism is based on the assumption that all physical effects have physical causes. Just because many physical effects have been found to have physical causes, does not mean that we can assume that all will. That is an unwarranted assumption.

Does a 'god of the gaps' get less likely as science advances? In fact, with the biological understanding of life, the advance of science has revealed a world of marvels unthought-of before. The 'gaps' or mysteries are getting greater![189]

False dualisms in criticism of ID by some Christians

1   Spiritual/Physical

It is alleged that Genesis 1 and other Biblical passages are 'spiritual' or 'theological' and not 'physical'. However Genesis 1 and other passages have as their subject God and the physical world. Theology is concerned, not only with the spiritual, but also with the physical. Hence, although the Resurrection of Christ had a spiritual dimension, it was nevertheless a Resurrection of the Body.

2   Creation/Redemption

Many Christians accept the miracles of Redemption as seen in Jesus but reject the Divine creative input expounded in Genesis 1. The Incarnation holds together Creation and Redemption and therefore they should not be treated as totally distinct.

ID makes no predictions as normal scientific theories do

This is a common criticism of ID. However it should be remembered that the theory of evolution makes no predictions either. That would be true of any theory which requires long periods of time in the past. Thinking of the present we should note the words of Jerry Coyne an evolutionary biologist writing in Nature. He acknowledges, in a recently published book review:

> If truth be told, evolution hasn't yielded many practical or commercial benefits... Evolution cannot help us predict what new vaccines to manufacture... Most improvement in crop plants and animals occurred long before we knew anything about evolution.[190]

---

[189] In his book *Shadows Of The Mind* Roger Penrose (retired Professor of Mathematics, Oxford) said: 'It should be made clear that science and mathematics have revealed a world full of mystery. The deeper that our scientific understanding becomes, the more the profound the mystery that is revealed. It is perhaps noteworthy that the physicists, who are more directly familiar with the puzzling and mysterious ways in which matter *actually* behaves, tend to take a less classically mechanistic view of the world than do some biologists.'

[190] Jerry A. Coyne, 'Selling Darwin', Nature 442 (2006): pp. 983-84.

It is 'immunised' (Karl Popper's phrase – see below) against such a test. Actually ID does make predictions. It predicts that there will always be a discontinuity between non-living matter and living matter. Exclusively physical properties between non-living matter and living matter will never be found. The basis of this prediction is that the DNA and RNA (essential to life) are a form of instruction or code – see section above entitled 'Mind and Matter'.

John Polkinghorne, although neutral on ID, says:

> Placing an extraordinary overconfidence in science's unaided power to gain understanding can lead some biologists to make grossly inflated claims that their insights are capable of explaining pretty well everything. Many physicists were in this kind of grandiose mood in the generations that followed Isaac Newton's great discoveries, but later discernment of the complex subtlety of physical processes eventually led that community to a more humble recognition that mechanism is not all. Man is more than a machine. Yet biologists today, in the wake of their stunning discoveries in molecular genetics, are all too prone to a euphoric degree of unjustified triumphalism that grossly exaggerates the explanatory power of their discipline. I feel sure that this temporary episode will not survive the recovery of full biological interest in organisms as well as in molecules.[191]

Karl Popper says evolution is not a scientific theory because it cannot be tested. He regards theories as 'immunised' as those that are protected against all future discoveries because they can be reconciled with anything.[192] His theory of falsification says that for a theory to be counted as scientific, the proposer must be able to stipulate what new facts if found in the future would falsify his theory. Evolution in its modern form fails this test and is 'immunised' against all possible future discoveries. He regards this as a bad thing. He says 'Evolution' is at best a philosophical framework in which other scientific disciplines can find their home. He therefore reluctantly accepted it.

But can evolution provide such a framework?

Two opinions

Not being in the same scientific league as many geneticists I cannot argue with their biology. However it is often said that Darwinian evolution provides the paradigm within which all biological research is carried out. For example Denis Alexander who has made his case against ID, says in his otherwise very good book *Rebuilding the Matrix* (page 289):

---

[191] *Exploring Reality* p. 137.
[192] *Unended Quest.*

The theory gives coherence to an immense varied array of research fields, including molecular biology, biochemistry, immunology, developmental biology, zoology, botany, anatomy anthropology, geology, ecology and behavioural psychology, to name but a few.

Now compare that statement with the following statement from Philip S. Skell, Member of the National Academy of Sciences, Evan Pugh Professor of Chemistry, Emeritus, Penn State University. He researched researchers. He asked them to consider a world where there was no theory of evolution. What difference would it have made to their research? In 2005 he said:

I recently asked more than 70 eminent researchers if they would have done their work differently if they had thought Darwin's theory was wrong. The responses were all the same: No.

I also examined the outstanding biodiscoveries of the past century: the discovery of the double helix; the characterization of the ribosome; the mapping of genomes; research on medications and drug reactions; improvements in food production and sanitation; the development of new surgeries; and others. I even queried biologists working in areas where one would expect the Darwinian paradigm to have most benefited research, such as the emergence of resistance to antibiotics and pesticides. Here, as elsewhere, I found that Darwin's theory had provided no discernible guidance, but was brought in, after the breakthroughs, as an interesting narrative gloss.

Many of the scientific criticisms [of neo-Darwinism] are well known by scientists in various disciplines, including the disciplines of chemistry and biochemistry, in which I have done my work. I have found that some of my scientific colleagues are very reluctant to acknowledge the existence of problems with evolutionary theory to the general public. They display an almost religious zeal for a strictly Darwinian view of biological origins. Darwinian evolution is an interesting theory about the remote history of life. Nonetheless, it has little practical impact on those branches of science that do not address questions of biological history (largely based on stones, the fossil evidence). Modern biology is engaged in the examination of tissues from living organisms with new methods and instruments. None of the great discoveries in biology and medicine over the past century depended on guidance from Darwinian evolution – it provided no support.[193]

---

[193] From his *Open Letter to the Kansas State Board of Education*, 2005

Dawkins[194] and the Origin of Complexity

So who made God? This question is the essence of Richard Dawkins' argument on page 141 of *The Blind Watchmaker*.[195]

He says a Creator, in order to make such a thing as the DNA would have to be at least as complex as the DNA. If we have to explain the origin of the DNA's complexity then we must explain the origin of the complexity of God.

What is wrong with this argument? It assumes that the laws of nature (i.e. cause and effect) apply to that which is beyond nature – a patently false assumption. If God exists then He is, by definition, beyond nature.

Dawkins goes on to say:

> You have to say something like 'God was always there', and if you allow yourself that sort of lazy way out, you might as well just say 'DNA was always there', or 'Life was always there' and be done with it.

Although, no doubt, Dawkins means this as a rhetorical sentence, its rhetoric can only be effective if the sentence makes any sense. But it doesn't. It is beyond dispute that DNA and life were not always there! No one pretends that they were. We do not know the laws that relate to the Eternal existence of God who is beyond nature, but what we do know is that life has not always existed.

It is a common claim of Richard Dawkins and others that a cause for nature's complexity must be more complex than nature itself. Thus that complex cause's existence must call for explanation. However is this true? For example a war between nations may be very complex, but the cause of the war may be one man's greed, jealousy or ambition. Just as we invoke non-complex but personal causes for complex situations, why not invoke a Personal cause for the existence of life?[196] Indeed Thomas Aquinas argues that God must be simple i.e. He must have no component parts.

---

[194] He admits life has 'an illusion of design so persuasive that it is almost impossible to distinguish from deliberate intelligent design'. (Article in the Guardian, 11th February 2008)

[195] The whole book is reviewed in www..apologetics.fsnet.co.uk/dawkins.htm.

[196] This is the essence of Keith Ward's argument in a Tablet article in January 2006.

Appendix 4

A Consideration of Roger Penrose's Use of Gödel's Theorem to Prove that the Mind must be more than a Complex Physical Mechanism

The purpose of this appendix is to consider the contribution of Roger Penrose to the discussion of consciousness and relate it to earlier discussions. Two of Penrose's best known books are *The Emperor's New Mind* and *Shadows of the Mind*.

Roger Penrose identifies four possible positions relating to consciousness:[197]

1   There is nothing to stop future technology producing conscious computers able to experience happiness and exercise such attributes as compassion.

2   Computers may be made that can exactly imitate consciousness but they will not really be conscious.

3   Understanding consciousness will require an entirely new science. However complex computers are made using our present understanding of science, they will never even be able to fully imitate consciousness never mind be actually conscious. A new – and as yet unknown science involving the understanding of a 'quantum computer' – will be necessary.

4   No science will understand human self-awareness because it lies in that realm which is beyond the physical world in the 'spiritual'.

Penrose claims to prove that 1 and 2 are impossible. He says he doesn't like 4 because of its mystical or religious overtones and so opts for 3. However some of his comments imply that he is moving in the direction of 4.

His proof makes use of Gödel's theorem and he shows that thinking and knowing are not things that could ever be reproduced by mechanical methods. First, we need to rehearse the nature of Gödel's theorem.

In the 1930s the German mathematician Kurt Gödel showed that there will always be statements in formal systems of mathematics that cannot be shown to be true or false from within those systems. Each system would start with the given axioms which could – applying fixed procedures of logic – be used to test certain theorems to decide or prove whether they were true or

---

[197]   Penrose Roger, 1994, *Shadows of the Mind*, p. 12.

false. He managed to translate statements *about* Mathematics into Mathematics itself. He then showed that it was possible to use Mathematics to say something about itself. He managed to number the statements in a formal system of Mathematics in such a way that statement number n said: 'Statement number n cannot be proved in the system.' *We* can see that this statement must be true, for if not, statement number n would have a proof, i.e. the system would contain a flat contradiction. The same is true if it could be disproved within the system: the system contains a true statement which it cannot prove or disprove. From an enlarged system – with more axioms and more procedures – it could be seen that 'n' is true or false. But that enlarged system again would itself contain its own undecidable statements, and so on . . .

Now computers use fixed procedures for doing their work (such as problem solving or accomplishing some other end) in a finite number of steps. This includes computers that learn from experience using neural networks because the learning processes of such computers themselves work according to pre-programmed procedures.

To paraphrase Penrose: the question is whether or not the human mind simply uses fixed procedures to establish logical or mathematical truths. If the workings of the mind are entirely algorithmic, then the procedures that I might actually use to form my conclusions are not capable of dealing with all the propositions constructed from the way my mind works. Nevertheless other people can (in principle) see that these – for me undecidable propositions – are actually true. This would seem to provide me with a mystery since I ought to be able to see that also. This is essentially the argument put forward by the philosopher Lucas (1961) that the mind's action cannot be entirely algorithmic. He argued, human beings have the ability to continually diagnose and correct their own limitations in a way to which there can be no parallel in machines.

Some have tried to refute Lucas's argument. Not least of these is the Artificial Intelligence expert Douglas Hofstadter in *Gödel, Escher, and Bach - an Eternal Golden Braid*. Although the book is indeed brilliant, the one part that I found unconvincing is his discussion and criticism of Lucas.[198] He quotes Lucas:

However complicated a machine we construct, it will, if it is a machine, correspond to a formal system, which in turn will be liable to the Gödel procedure of finding a formula unprovable-in-that-system. This formula the machine will be unable to produce as being true, although a mind can see it is true. And so the machine will still not be an adequate model of the mind. We

---

[198] Hofstadter D.R., 1980, *Gödel Escher and Bach*, pp. 470ff.

are trying to produce a model of the mind which is mechanical - which is essentially 'dead' – but the mind being in fact 'alive', can always go one better than any formal, ossified, dead system can. Thanks to Gödel's theorem, the mind always has the last word.

Hofstadter's response is really to say that even minds are vulnerable to Gödel's theorem. He approvingly cites C.H. Whitely whom he quotes as saying that 'Lucas cannot consistently assert this sentence'.[199] Here is a sentence: 'The mind always has the last word'; Hofstadter tells us that is true but Lucas cannot consistently assert it. But have Hofstadter and Whitely won the point? Surely not. The reason that Lucas cannot reasonably assert the sentence is that for Lucas to attempt to assert it would be manifestly absurd. Not only can *we* see that it is absurd but *Lucas can as well*. Thus at this point Lucas's reasoning has not itself been trapped by Gödel's theorem.

A few pages earlier[200] Hofstadter argues that even though the procedures that mathematicians use to decide the theorems are very very complex – much more complex than that of known computers – they are still ultimately vulnerable to Gödel's theorem. So then he argues that the human mind has no advantage in principle over computers. But Penrose has a response which I believe is compelling. He points out that human mathematical reasoning is not complex. Each step in any mathematical argument can be reduced to something 'simple and obvious'. The most simple and obvious truths and procedures – upon which all Mathematics is ultimately built – are simply perceived to be true by *conscious* beings. They are not reached by formal logical reasoning. They are 'seen' by the conscious mind. So he concludes that 'Mathematical truth is not something we ascertain merely by use of an algorithm.'

He goes on:

I believe, also, that our consciousness is a crucial ingredient in our comprehension of mathematical truth. We must 'see' the truth of mathematical argument to be convinced of its validity. This 'seeing' is the very essence of consciousness. It must be present whenever we directly perceive mathematical truth. When we convince ourselves of the validity of Gödel's theorem we not only 'see' it, but by so doing we reveal the very non-algorithmic nature of the 'seeing' process itself.[201]

---

199   *Gödel Escher and Bach*, p. 477.
200   *Gödel Escher and Bach*, p. 475.
201   Penrose Roger, 1989, *The Emperor's New Mind*, p. 541.

John Puddefoot reflecting on the same subject says:

An 'inside-out' life must be the centre of new creative ideas and that it resource its own ideas by looking for and hungering for new input stimuli. An inside-out perspective initiates searches for new information, and the nature of those searches (what it looks for, how it proceeds, what it selects and what it rejects, how it deals with and responds to chance encounters with interesting, relevant and irrelevant material) are indications of the kind of 'person' the inside-out-ness is constituted by.[202]

This way of discerning truth independent of fixed procedures is the subject of a discussion of scientific method by Lesslie Newbigin in *The Gospel and Modern Culture* pages 30ff. He quotes Bertrand Russell who sums up what he believes is the scientific way of learning and knowing:

In arriving at a scientific law there are three main stages: the first consists of observing the significant facts; the second in arriving at a hypothesis which, if true, would account for the facts; the third in deducing from this hypothesis consequences which can be tested by observation.[203]

Newbigin goes on to follow the argument of Drusilla Scott, *Everyman Revived: The Common Sense of Michael Polanyi*. Here is a shortened version of it.

First, how do we know what are the **significant** facts? There are billions of facts lying around. The scientist has to identify the facts that are significant for the problem he wants to solve. That is a matter for personal judgement and there are no rules for deciding it. Then he must identify a 'good problem'. Years have been wasted in the attempt to solve problems which led nowhere. A good scientist is one who can identify a good problem. But what is a good problem? The answer seems to be that to recognise a problem is to sense, by a kind of intuition, that there is something to be discovered which has not yet fully revealed itself but of which there are hints. Einstein said:

The supreme task of the physicist is the search of those highly universal laws from which a picture of the world can be obtained by pure deduction. There is no logical path leading to these laws. They are only to be reached by intuition, based upon something like an intellectual love.[204]

Second, how is a hypothesis composed? Again there are no rules. It is much more a matter of intuition and imagination. Some of the most significant theories have come from a vision or dream. The immensely creative

---

[202] Puddefoot John, 1996, *God and the Mind Machine*, p. 113.
[203] *The Scientific Outlook*, p. 58.
[204] *The World as I see it*, p. 125.

generalisations first formulated by Newton and by Einstein were in no sense the result of a process which could be described in terms of rules or fixed procedures. Einstein is recorded as expressing his delight when the poet St John Perse spoke to him of the importance of intuition in poetry. 'But the same thing is true for the man of science,' he said; 'The mechanics of discovery are neither logical nor intellectual. It's a sudden illumination, almost a rapture. Later, to be sure, intelligence and analysis and experiment confirm the intuition. But initially there is a great leap of the imagination.'

Roger Penrose himself gives interesting and moving accounts from his own life and other scientists such as Dirac (of quantum theory) showing how inspiration and sudden illumination – when the mind seemed engrossed in an entirely different and perhaps trivial subject – brought great insight and advance in scientific understanding.

In *Shadows of the Mind* he uses more rigorous proofs from Gödel's theorem that real knowledge cannot be reduced to mechanical reasoning, however full it is of complexity and self-learning, and self-referential processes. Even, he says, if randomness were introduced into a computer (with unpredictable radioactive decay) it would not escape Gödel.[205] Yet even with all his high maths and deep philosophical arguments Penrose acknowledges that what he is arguing is only what is obvious to any child!

Yet beneath all this technicality is the feeling that it is indeed 'obvious' that the conscious mind cannot work like a computer, even though much of what is actually involved in mental activity might do so.

This is the kind of obviousness that a child can see – though that child may, in later life, become browbeaten into believing that the obvious problems are 'non-problems':

> We often forget the wonder that we felt as children, before the cares of the 'real world' have begun to settle upon our shoulders. Children are not afraid to pose the basic questions that may embarrass us, as adults, to ask. What happens to each of our streams of consciousness after we die . . . why are we here; why is there a universe here at all in which we can actually be?[206]

It is Plato to whom Penrose often turns. Plato's view is that as well as a physical world there is also a timeless world of ideas which is real but without physical location.

---

[205] *Shadows of the Mind*, p. 154.
[206] Penrose Roger, 1989, *The Emperor's New Mind*, p. 578ff.

How is it that mathematical ideas can be communicated in this way? I imagine that whenever the mind perceives a mathematical idea, it makes contact with Plato's world of mathematical concepts. When one 'sees' a mathematical truth one's consciousness breaks through into this world of ideas, and makes direct contact with it. I have described this 'seeing' in relation to Gödel's theorem, but it is the essence of mathematical understanding. When mathematicians communicate, this is made possible by each one having a direct route to truth, the consciousness of each being in a position to perceive mathematical truths directly , through this process of 'seeing'. (indeed, often this act of perception is accompanied by words like 'Oh I see'!). Since each can make contact with Plato's world directly, they can more readily communicate with each other that one might have expected. The mental images that each one has, when making this Platonic contact, might be rather different in each case, but communication is possible because each is directly in contact with the same externally existing Platonic world![207]

Much earlier in *The Emperor's New Mind* Penrose asks:

Is Mathematics invention or discovery? When mathematicians come upon their results are they just producing elaborated mental constructions which have no actual reality, but whose power and elegance is sufficient simply to fool even their inventors into believing that these mere mental constructions are 'real'? Or are mathematicians really uncovering truths which are, in fact, already 'there' — truths whose existence is quite independent of the mathematicians' activities? I think that, by now, it must be quite clear to the reader that I am an adherent of the second, rather than the first view, at least with regard to such structures as complex numbers and the Mandelbrot set.[208]

If mathematics were just the human invention of symbols to be manipulated by rules it is difficult to explain how mathematicians find delight in the beauty of theorems their work leads them to. Penrose says to us:

Great works of art are indeed 'closer to God' than are lesser ones. It is a feeling not uncommon amongst artists, that in their greatest works they are revealing eternal truths which have some kind of prior ethereal existence, while their lesser works might be more arbitrary, of the nature of mere mortal constructions. Likewise, an engineering innovation with a beautiful economy, where a great deal is achieved in the scope of the application of some simple, unexpected idea, might appropriately be described as a discovery rather than an invention.[209]

---

[207] *The Emperor's New Mind*, p. 554.
[208] *The Emperor's New Mind*, p. 126.
[209] *The Emperor's New Mind*, p. 127.

Are we being forced in the direction of Cartesian dualism?

Cartesians following Descartes divide the world into a metaphysical dualism of two finite substances, mind (spirit or soul) and matter. The essence of mind is self-conscious thinking, the essence of matter is extension in three dimensions. God is a third, infinite substance, whose essence is necessary existence, and God unites minds with bodies to create a fourth, compound substance – a human being. Humans have general knowledge of mind, matter, and God by contemplating innate ideas.

For particular knowledge of events in the world, however, humans depend on motions, transmitted from the sense organs through nerves to the brain, that cause sensible ideas to arise in the mind. Cartesians thus claimed to know the outer world by way of representative sensible ideas in the mind.

But the dualist is faced with the question of how, if at all, mind and matter are related to each other.

There are various ways that dualists have proposed to account for the relationship. The most straightforward position is interactionism, the view (held by Descartes) that mind and body are capable of affecting each other causally, so that what happens in the body can produce effects in the mind and vice versa. Descartes decided that somewhere within the nerve tissues of the brain was the place where the interactions occurred and chose the pineal gland as the precise point because of its central location. (It is now known that the pineal gland cannot perform the functions that Descartes attributed to it, though its precise functions are still unknown.)

Two hundred and fifty years later Penrose himself speculates at length that an understanding of the brain's neurones, synapses, cytoskelitons, and microtubules might help us as to where quantum action in the brain might take place.[210] This however is the least satisfactory part of his book and even if he is right it leaves unanswered the main issues of the subjective nature of self-awareness which he himself raises.[211]

Among the difficulties of dualism is the inherent obscurity in conceiving of what sort of thing a mental substance – an immaterial, 'thinking stuff' – might be.

---

[210] *Shadows of the Mind*, the whole of chapter 7.

[211] David Chalmers also makes this same point against Penrose in his article: 'The Puzzle of Conscious Experience' in a special issue of 'Scientific American' entitled 'Mysteries of the Mind'.

Arthur Peacocke believes that human consciousness has emerged from the biological complexity of the brain but cannot be reduced to biology alone. He believes in various layers of being. The higher emerge from the lower but then take on a life of their own and cannot be reduced to a mere quality of that lower level. For example biology is more than chemistry which itself is more than physics. At a certain level of complexity new levels of being emerge which, taking on a life of their own, cannot be understood simply in terms of that from which they have emerged.[212] But does consciousness just emerge at a certain point of complexity of the nervous system, or need it be called forth?

John Haldane argues that self-replicating molecules such as RNA and DNA comprise a case of 'radical emergence'[213] which cannot be understood in terms of a naturalist theory of evolution. From the points I have made I further have to agree with him that the emergence of consciousness, also, is a 'radical emergence' which is by definition not compatible with a naturalist theory of evolution but requires 'creative intelligence'.[214]

Ernest Lucas writes:

There is a human spirit, made in the image of its Creator, which, though expressed through the material body, is not to be simply identified with it.

---

[212] A. R. Peacocke, *Creation and the World of Science*, 1979, pp. 112-31.

[213] Colin McGinn distinguishes two main types of emergence and clearly believes that consciousness is an example of what some call 'radical emergence'. He says, 'I might summarise our cognitive predicament by distinguishing two types of novelty that the world may contain. Type 1 novelty . . . applies to linguistic novelty and to the sort of novelty that results when material particles are arranged in various ways. It is fundamentally combinatorial, iterative, and transparent. Type 2 novelty is the kind that cannot be regarded in this way, and which therefore invites the epithet 'genuine': the emergence of consciousness from the brain is a case in point. It is just when we find ourselves reaching for ideas of type 2 novelty with the attendant notions of radical emergence, underdetermination and irreducible duality that we are entering philosophical territory. And a characteristic response to the consequent bafflement is an attempt (always doomed) to construe a type 2 case as really a type 1 case, as with typical domesticating projects. We have a natural drive towards the combinatorial, so we try to assimilate everything to that, frequently distorting reality in the process.' (Italics added) (http://www.nyu.edu/gsas/dept/philo/courses/consciousness/papers/ProblemOfPhilosophy.html)

[214] Atheism and Theism, by J.J.C. Smart and J. J. Haldane, pp. 195-99 and also J. J. Haldane 'The Mystery of Emergence' in Proceedings of the Aristotelian Society, Vol. 96, Pt 2, 1996. See also Michael Degnan's very useful discussion of this in his review article in Zygon, December 1996.

This, however, does not mean acceptance of a sharp Cartesian dualism. This 'spirit' need not be thought of as another 'bit' which could be discovered along with the other bits by a reductionist methodology. It is more like the meaning of this paragraph. The meaning is to be identified with the letters, which carry it. No amount of study of the individual letters, or even words, in isolation will reveal the existence of the meaning. It can be found only when the paragraph is taken as a whole. Of course the meaning will disappear if the letters are erased. However, it will not cease to exist, because it still exists in my mind. I can express it again perhaps in different letters (Greek or Hebrew).

My own view is something similar to the interactionism of Descartes, Penrose, Karl Popper and John Eccles.[215] I do believe the soul exists and interacts causally with the body and is not merely a certain property of the body. However I also believe that soul and body are not complete in themselves but each needs the other to form a true human being. Are they then two substances? It is a great mystery because even the nature of 'material stuff' which makes the body is a mystery.[216] Thus I prefer the word 'duality' to 'dualism' to describe my view.

Quantum theory itself teaches us that elementary building blocks of matter cannot be themselves be confined to one place at one time. Penrose again:

Quantum theory seems to tell us that material particles are merely 'waves of information' . . . Thus matter itself is nebulous and transient.[217]

So the whole of material existence is related at its foundation to a system of information which breaks the common sense rules of space and time. So it is not as if there are two substances necessarily but rather that what we think of as the material comes forth from information. Once we admit information we are getting near to language, meaning, purpose, and logos. It seems reasonable to believe that since personal beings have arisen in the universe the logos from whom all things have their being cannot be less than a personal Word of Life. Either this Word of Life is simply the cosmic consciousness of all of nature (the Pantheist view) or He is the Creator and Sustainer of all things (the Biblical view). One problem with the Pantheist position is that if we are all parts of God then how do we account for the enormous reality of evil and the genuine experiences of both freedom and alienation?

Roger Penrose claims he is not arguing for anything religious – his belief that science always triumphs stops him from that. However his argument

---

215 Popper's and Eccles' view is marvellously described in *The Self and Its Brain*, 1977, by Popper and Eccles.
216 This was pointed out earlier in this book in the discussion: 'What is matter?'
217 Penrose Roger, 1994, *Shadows of the Mind*, p. 14.

inevitably must lead him in that direction. He argues that consciousness is the link between the quantum world, in which a single object can exist in two places at the same time, and the so-called classical world of familiar objects where this cannot happen. The most dominant view among theoretical physicists is that quantum mechanics and consciousness are linked on the principle that the act of measurement – which ultimately has to involve a **conscious** observer – has an effect on quantum events. So if the mind is a quantum computer depending on consciousness itself, we still have not started solving the problem of consciousness from physics. Further the conviction that the basis of all matter is some form of consciousness must surely lead to a religious quest.

Consciousness seems to me to be such an important phenomenon that I simply cannot believe that it is something just 'accidentally' conjured up by a complicated computation. It is the phenomenon whereby the universe's very existence is made known. One can argue that a universe governed by laws that do not allow consciousness is no universe at all. I would even say that all the mathematical descriptions of a universe that have been given so far must fail this criterion. It is only the phenomenon of consciousness that can conjure a putative 'theoretical' universe into actual existence![218]

How does the Platonic world relate to the physical world?

. . . minds could seem to manifest some mysterious connection between the physical world and Plato's world.[219]

But why *Plato's* world? His eternal world of forms was unchanging and therefore impersonal. Would it not be more reasonable to believe that our mind's understanding of mathematics points to a transcendent mathematics which has its origin in a conscious and therefore *personal* Mind?

It seems to me that we are not far from the Biblical worldview that humans, made in the image of God, are the link between God and the natural world. We are meant to voice the praise of all of nature to God and represent God in caring for the world which He has entrusted to our care.

For further material, see the author's website:
www.hgtaylor.net/questions-answers.htm

---

[218] Penrose Roger, 1989 *The Emperor's New Mind*, pp. 579-80.
[219] *The Emperor's New Mind*, p. 557.